TEAMMATE

TEAMMATE

My Journey in Baseball and a
World Series for the Ages

DAVID ROSS
with Don Yaeger

hachette
BOOKS
NEW YORK   BOSTON

I am looking forward to the next chapters in my life and growing with my team, Team Ross. I thank God for all of you, Hyla, Landri, Cole, and Harper. DR

To Jeanette, Will, and Maddie—my mates in the most important team of all: home. DY

Hachette Books
Hachette Book Group
1290 Avenue of the Americas
New York, NY 10104
hachettebooks.com
twitter.com/hachettebooks

First Edition: May 2017

Hachette Books is a division of Hachette Book Group, Inc.
The Hachette Books name and logo are trademarks of Hachette Book Group, Inc.

The publisher is not responsible for websites (or their content) that are not owned by the publisher.

The Hachette Speakers Bureau provides a wide range of authors for speaking events.
To find out more, go to www.hachettespeakersbureau.com or call (866) 376-6591.

Library of Congress Control Number: 2017934155

ISBNs: 978-0-316-55944-7 (hardcover), 978-0-316-47221-0 (signed edition),
978-0-316-55942-3 (ebook)

Printed in the United States of America

LSC-C

10 9 8 7 6 5 4 3 2 1

CONTENTS

FOREWORD ix

PREFACE xvii

CHAPTER 1: **"This Wasn't About Me"** 1

CHAPTER 2: **Time for a Nap** 17

CHAPTER 3: **Ball Bags.** 27

CHAPTER 4: **First Pitch** 39

CHAPTER 5: **Punch in the Gut** 55

CHAPTER 6: **Best Seat in the House** 69

CHAPTER 7: **Mike Napoli at the Plate.** 81

CHAPTER 8: **Contreras off the Wall** 97

CHAPTER 9: **Just Continue to Breathe** 111

CHAPTER 10: **Call to the Bullpen** 123

CHAPTER 11: **A Crazy Five Minutes** 139

CHAPTER 12: **Small Redemption** 155

CHAPTER 13: **High Anxiety** 171

CHAPTER 14: **Rain Delay** 185

CHAPTER 15: **Cubs Win, Cubs Win.** 199

CHAPTER 16: **Homecoming** 211

CHAPTER 17: **Wrigley** 227

EPILOGUE 235

ACKNOWLEDGMENTS 241

FOREWORD

I f this story had been submitted as a Hollywood script, it would have been rejected immediately as too corny, too unlikely, too impossible to believe. An aging backup catcher, in the final year of his career, wins over an entire fan base with the force of his personality and helps mold a young team into the very best in baseball. He hits a home run in Game Seven of the World Series and gets carried off the field by his teammates, a retiring hero on top of the world. Impossible to believe? Perhaps, but not for those lucky enough to know David Ross.

I first got to know David in August 2008 at what was likely the nadir of his career. He had just been released by the Cincinnati Reds despite being in the middle of a multiyear contract. He was hitting just .231, but that's not the entire reason the Reds had decided to let David go. There were whispers out of Cincinnati that he was not a good teammate—that he was having a hard time accepting a diminished role and had become a bit of a headache for management. Others I trusted swore by David as "a great guy and a really smart player," but the whispers grew louder and David was released.

At the time we were looking to add catching depth to a Red Sox roster that featured veteran backstops Jason Varitek and Kevin Cash and was on the way to its fifth postseason appearance in six years. We had traded Manny Ramirez for Jason Bay weeks earlier to improve the unity in the clubhouse and had a good, solid, talented, professional club. Comforted by those who vouched for him and in need of a veteran "break glass in case of emergency" third catcher, we ignored the whispers and signed David. In full candor, I didn't expect much from him. I thought he would catch a game or two over the remainder of the season, sit on the bench during the postseason, and move on to the next stop of his career without making much of an impression or impact.

Well, I was right on the first two points. David had just eight at-bats over the final six weeks of the regular season and none in the playoffs. But, man, was I wrong about David not making an impact. Despite being the new guy on the team, despite hardly playing, despite suffering through a tough season, David was adored by his teammates and somehow found his way into the middle of our clubhouse dynamic.

By the time the playoffs came around, he was respected enough that we invited him into our advance scouting meetings along with Varitek and Cash. Again, I didn't expect much from David. These are big, important meetings with the front office, manager Terry Francona, and the whole coaching staff. Typically, advance scout Dana LeVangie and Varitek—both expert in this role—would take the lead breaking down opposing hitters, and pitching coach John Farrell, Tito, and a few of us in the front office would chime in. The third-string catcher was not usually present, let alone vocal. Except for David. He spoke up early and often, in a strong and authoritative voice, making insightful points about every opposing hitter. He wasn't afraid to disagree, even with Varitek, and quickly won over the room. By the third or fourth hitter we discussed, others were deferring to Ross, the backup's backup who up until the last six weeks had spent his entire career in the other league.

"That was impressive," I remember telling Assistant General Manager Jed Hoyer. "We should keep an eye on him . . . might make a good scout or coach when he's done playing." A couple of weeks later, the day after our demoralizing season-ending loss to the Tampa Bay Rays in Game Seven of the American League Championship Series, David and his teammates were cleaning out their lockers at Fenway Park. I asked to speak to him in private.

"Look, David, you were terrific on this team; everyone loved having you around. I don't know exactly what went down in Cincinnati, but there are some things you should know. You were getting a bit of a bad reputation over there—not the greatest teammate, not accepting of your role, a bit of a pain in the ass for everybody. That doesn't sound like you, but it wasn't from just one person and I thought you would want to know. You can still do a lot of things on the field: you have power, you can hit left-handed pitching, you can catch and throw, you can break down hitters. You can play a long time, but you profile best as a backup at this point and you have to accept that. And that means being a great teammate and doing whatever is necessary to help the team win. You're a free agent; I just thought you would want to hear what's being said about you. Thanks for what you did for us."

And that was that. I've had many similar conversations with other players over the years; it was nothing remarkable. I expected

David to kick around as a backup for a few more years before retiring. Maybe then we would make the call to see if he was ready to try scouting or coaching. Yet again, I made the mistake of underestimating David Ross.

Six years later, I was looking for a catcher again. Besides that, everything had changed. I was in Chicago, not Boston, and we had just signed Jon Lester to help turn a young, talented team into a contender. David had spent four years as a prolific backup catcher with the Atlanta Braves, making real contributions as a fine two-way player and becoming one of manager Bobby Cox's go-to veteran leaders in the clubhouse. Then, in a two-year stint back with the Red Sox, he was at the epicenter of the band of bearded brothers who galvanized a region after the Boston Marathon Bombing and won the 2013 World Series. David only caught 36 games during the season, but, remarkably, his manager and his teammates demanded that he be on the field when things mattered most during the Fall Classic. David caught all four of Boston's wins in the World Series. By this point he was well established as a great teammate and leader, someone thoughtful about winning and willing to put in the work to make it happen. With Lester's urging, we signed David despite having two productive catchers on the roster.

What is there to say about David's time with the Cubs? Some of it happened in plain sight. The tough year with the bat in 2015 that had many talk-show callers seeking his release. The tremendous job he did handling Lester and neutralizing the running game. The bounce-back offensive season in 2016 and the clutch home runs in October. Game Seven disaster and Game Seven triumph. The unconditional love of his teammates and the ride on their shoulders off the field for the last time.

But so much of David's impact on the Cubs went unseen. The late-night conversations with struggling teammates. The team dinners on the road to build morale and connection. The kind gestures to teammates who were new or didn't feel like part of the group. The thorough physical, mental, fundamental, and strategic preparation for each game. The expectation that his teammates do the same. The watchful eye from the dugout to make sure we respected the game and played the Cub Way—unselfish, team-first, winning-first baseball. The glare when someone did something that wasn't Cub. The rare harsh word when it happened again. The high-fives and pats on the rear when it got fixed. The instinct to know when to create levity and when to get guys locked in. Reminding the young players how good they are. Reminding them they can get better. Words to keep the team grounded when winning seemed easy. Words to lift up the team when losing just one more would end the season.

Unselfishness. Accountability. Connectedness. David was the catalyst for these winning ingredients because he studied them and went out of his way to cultivate them for his teammates. In some ways he was born for the role. He was friendly, funny, caring, and magnetic, so everyone wanted to be around him. But he could also be edgy, stubborn, and authoritative, so nobody dared question him. In other ways David grew into the responsibility. He studied the winning teams he played for and the ways the manager and veterans handled the clubhouse. He never wanted to be called a bad teammate again and prioritized winning and the group above all else.

Getting to know David and witnessing his evolution was one of the joys of my career. I will never forget sitting forward in my seat in 2008 when he took over the playoff meeting as a newcomer. Nor will I forget reveling in his storybook farewell season and the look on his face as his teammates carried him off the field a champion. With his character and commitment, Rossy helped take the team and me to great places. I am confident he will do the same for you as you read about his journey on these pages. You will find lessons for sports and for life, including one he helped teach me long ago: Never underestimate the power of a great teammate.

Especially when it's David Ross.

Theo Epstein
President of Baseball Operations, Chicago Cubs
February 2017

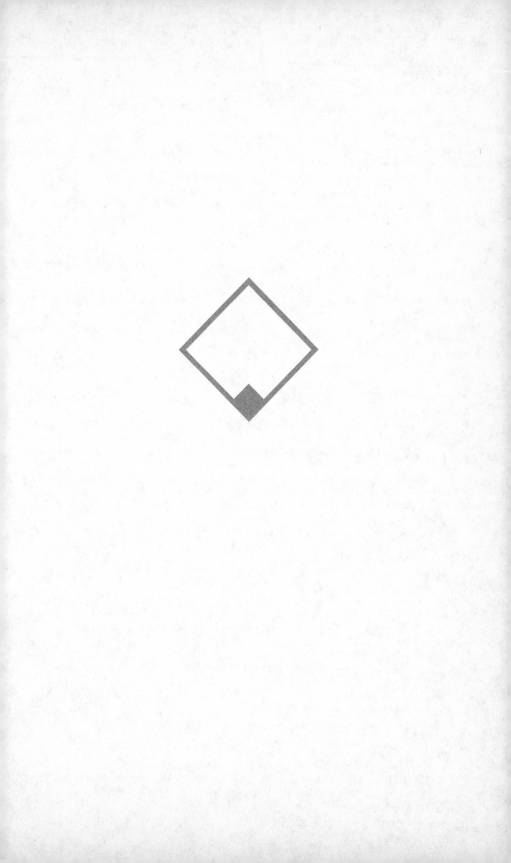

PREFACE

There have been days since November 2, 2016—the date my Chicago Cubs teammates and I won the World Series in the greatest Game Seven in history—when I have had to pinch myself. Incredible doesn't even begin to capture the feeling.

I knew coming into the 2016 season that it would be my last as a player in professional baseball. I also knew I was on a team that was loaded with talent and was, from the opening day, the favorite to win the Series. It took a lot for true Cubs fans to believe those oddsmakers. I mean for 108 years the Cubs have left those fans brokenhearted. Could this team really do it? Selfishly, could I get the chance to go out having won rings in both Chicago and Boston?

Knowing this was it, I did a number of things in this last season I had never done. I made it a point throughout the year to enjoy the cities we traveled to—I toured New York, played golf at Pebble Beach, made the most of towns I really only had a hotel-room view of in the past. I was lucky that my family could travel with me far more than in any year since my wife and I had children. I also found an app on my phone that allowed me to keep notes, and I'll be sharing entries from that "iPhone Journal" throughout this book.

But the biggest thing I did was reflect.

As it happened, a friend of mine, longtime *Sports Illustrated* writer Don Yaeger, caught me during one of those reflective moments with a crazy idea—maybe it was time to write a book. I have to admit, when Don mentioned the idea I was scared. I have seen people write books and it ruined the reputation they worked hard to build. That is the last thing I wanted to do. But the more the 2016 season went on and I received so much credit for things that others have taught me, I knew this was something I had to do. Key point here: This is a book about how people along the way affected me and helped me become a better teammate.

The idea of me writing a book might have, on some days, seemed ridiculous. Who would buy a book from a longtime backup catcher, right? But the idea Don came up with made sense. See, for all but a short stint of my career I have been a backup. I have never been an All-Star, never led my team in any offensive category. But my career was marked, especially over the last few years, by constant effort to get better both on the field and off. You see, because of an eye-opening experience with Theo Epstein, I made the effort a number of years ago to focus on being a great teammate. Then I went out and worked hard every day to be exactly that.

That's another key point—being a great teammate is work, hard work. It requires intention and discipline, just like becoming a better hitter or a better salesperson. But it is a skill set that I believe others, like me, can learn. Don's idea was that this book be about exactly that, passing along all that I've learned from others on an important subject: how to make yourself valuable, even if you're not the most valuable. You see, the teammate I am today is not who I was fifteen years ago! I have tried to take how others have made me feel and use that feeling, good or bad, to be a better teammate. I have learned from some of the best, and share these stories about them here to say thank you for investing in me.

I agreed to write the book way back in the beginning of the 2016 season.

Then the magic carpet ride just kept going. The Cubs kept exceeding even the wild expectations that were being thrown out there and we were having fun doing it. The team's enthusiasm became infectious, even to people who might not otherwise have been fans. I heard regularly how people enjoyed watching us enjoy working with each other.

Of all sports, I believe baseball has the greatest connection to the "real" world. It is a grind. If your team is good, you will still lose sixty times in a season. If you're good offensively, you will still fail more than seven of every ten times you get a chance to do your job. To be successful as a team or as an individual, you have to be able to manage through lots of "dog days." Imagine having to be encouraging to others while fighting through that grind as a backup! To be honest with everyone around you, humble no matter how good things get, reliable and consistent so that everyone knows what to expect, to willingly share your experiences with others—including those who might one day take your job!—to manage change with a smile on your face and stay engaged with everyone so that you can know how best to inspire them.

That is what it takes to be a great teammate.

Here's hoping that as you read this book you'll have fun hearing my stories and reliving the magic of the 2016 season. Just as important, I hope you take something away from the book about how to be a good teammate. That's why I wrote it.

David Ross

February 2017

TEAMMATE

CHAPTER 1

"THIS WASN'T ABOUT ME"

9:30 A.M.

From the moment I began to stir in bed on the morning of Wednesday, November 2, 2016, my mind was already racing. While most of America was at work, I was finally waking up. After leaving the locker room and winding down, I finally got to bed the night before at 2 a.m. as our Chicago Cubs continued chasing one of the great dreams in all of sports—one that had eluded us for more than one hundred years: winning another World Series.

My wife and two of my three children were with me in Cleveland, Ohio. Our infant daughter, Harper, was in Chicago with my parents, who had traveled from Tallahassee, Florida, beginning with the National League Division Series almost a month earlier. We arrived in Cleveland two nights earlier, checking into a suite at the Westin.

The suite was an exceptionally generous season-long retirement gift from my Cubs teammate Jason Heyward. The gift covered all thirty road trips the Cubs made during the 2016 season and it allowed me to comfortably spend quality time with my family during the season. In my previous fourteen years in the major leagues, I usually stayed in a standard single room provided by the team.

This particular Westin was beautiful, a few blocks from the Lake Erie waterfront and Progressive Field in downtown Cleveland. As I opened my eyes and looked around the hotel room, I saw my wife, Hyla; my seven-year-old son, Cole; and my nine-year-old daughter, Landri. Here I was, with my family, and it was suddenly dawning on me that this would be my final morning waking as a major-league baseball player. I was thirty-nine years old—truly ancient in professional sports—and had been in the majors for fifteen years, the last two with the Cubs.

My journey to this point in professional baseball was an improbable roller coaster—almost too good to be true. I was a catcher who had the talent to make it to the majors. But making it is one thing. After being tapped by the Dodgers in the seventh round of the 1998 draft, I finally made by big league debut in 2002. I would go on to play for seven different teams and spend the majority of my career as a backup. I was never an All-Star. My career batting average was .229—nothing to brag about. When I was released by the Cincinnati Reds in 2008, I thought my career was over. I suffered a series of severe concussions with the Boston Red Sox in 2013 that sidelined me, leaving me wondering if I would ever recover and return to playing.

Every new contract was a struggle, but somehow I kept going, year after year, and teams kept offering me the chance to live my dream.

Truth be told, I wasn't always the best teammate, especially in the early years. Like a lot of guys, I was seduced by the hype of being a professional baseball player.

But in time I managed to learn a few lessons. I learned how I wanted to treat people—not only on my team, but in life. I learned the importance of accountability and being invested in every one of your teammates. I realized character could be as valuable as a home run, and my behavior and that attitude helped extend my career.

But on that Wednesday morning in Cleveland, all of that was far from my mind. Today wasn't about me.

Less than ten hours earlier, we had beaten the Cleveland Indians 9–3 in Game Six to tie the best-of-seven series at three games apiece. The first pitch for Game Seven at Progressive Field was ten and a half hours away. It had been 108 years since the Cubs won their last title, and the generations of heartbreak for Cubs fans had little by little over the course of the season transformed from disbelief into real hope that this would be the season.

But that wasn't on my mind, either. What was?

I needed a Starbucks. Desperately.

I actually had gotten up five hours earlier with Cole because he didn't feel well. The kids had been battling illness over the last few days and Hyla was exhausted. When I got up the second time, around 9:30 a.m., I tried to go back to sleep but I couldn't. I turned on the television and channel surfed. I wanted to watch a game show or some reality show, anything that would have allowed me to turn off my brain. I was already beginning to feel nerves about that night's game.

All the networks were in full coverage mode. It seemed as if every channel or station I flipped on had their reporters in downtown Cleveland and at Progressive Field with breathless "Live Reports." Everyone had an opinion on Game Seven. The last thing I cared about was anybody else's opinion on our game. I knew the mindset of our team, what was being said in the clubhouse, and what we needed to do. I turned off the television.

I grabbed my iPhone next and mindlessly flipped through Twitter, but that didn't help, either. Everyone's thoughts—even at 140 characters—were on the game, too. Cole was now awake and playing on his iPad, while Hyla and Landri caught a few more winks.

It was still morning in our suite, but my mind was now jackhammer, midafternoon awake. I threw on a T-shirt, sweatpants, and flip-flops and went downstairs to the Starbucks in the hotel. The lobby was chaos. People were everywhere, and the place was loaded with Cubs fans who had come to be part of history. Some of them recognized me and came up to wish the team and me good luck. They marveled at how cool the season-long journey had been to bring us to this place. Everyone was so nice and I loved seeing all the positive energy. But some of the people who approached me wanted to make the day about me, noting my impending retirement. That's what I didn't want.

I was humbled—and overwhelmed at times—by all the attention. For most of fourteen seasons, I was a backup catcher. Sure, I signed autographs and hard-core fans would sometimes recognize me on the street. But it was nothing like what happened in 2016. Somehow my final season had turned into a year-long retirement party. I was no longer David Ross, but thirty-nine-year-old "Grandpa Rossy"—to my teammates and fans alike.

I still struggled to believe the series of events that season. It had all started in spring training when a few of my teammates said some nice things about me. Anthony Rizzo and Kris Bryant took things viral when they opened and named the "Grandpa Rossy" Instagram account and the Cubs communications staff snapped a few photographs of me to help them get it started. A year later the site has more than three hundred thousand followers. It still makes me smile!

The Chicago fans read everything and they quickly joined in. I absolutely had no idea why I was so beloved by fans, but it made for an incredible final season. There were so many times during the season I was brought to tears by everyone's generosity and kind words.

But now, standing in the hotel lobby in Cleveland, the last thing I wanted to hear was something about me. I said it to anyone who would listen: I didn't want my last day in baseball to be a distraction for anyone, least of all me!

I bought coffee for Hyla and me—and a big ol' donut for the kids—and headed back to the room. I usually let Landri and Cole split a donut, but I'm not supposed to. Hyla doesn't want the kids to eat donuts for breakfast. But, hey, I figured since it was Game Seven we could break a rule. Back in the room, Landri nibbled at the donut, and then even though Cole wasn't very hungry, he accompanied me back downstairs for a second breakfast in a banquet room decked out with a buffet for players and their families.

It was time to go see the team.

• • • • • • • • • • • • • • •

DAVID'S iPHONE JOURNAL
1/30/16

I was talking with some friends one night about retiring and how I wanted to take things in much more this year. I don't want the great moments to be forgotten as soon as the next one comes. They said I should start a journal, so here we go. Knowing this is my last year, the off-season has been like no other. I have been on an emotional roller coaster since Christmas. I've been doing a lot of reflecting on my career and the people I've come in contact with over the years. The other night I put on the 2013 World Series video and laughed/cried till I went to bed. I'm feeling way more appreciative for others who have helped in my journey and have supported me through the highs and lows. A guy like Steve Givens who has been throwing BP to me at night anytime I ask since high school. Freezing cold, 10:00 at night, after a full day's work and an hour car ride, and never asked for anything. He has been my sounding board and giving me great advice many a night.

．．．．．．．．．．．．．．．．

I grew up in Tallahassee. It's a nice city, the state capital, and it's located in the northern panhandle, about thirty minutes from the Georgia–Florida state line. It's an educational hub, too, with Florida State University, Florida A&M University, and Tallahassee Community College all within five miles of each other. There's tons to do year-round. The closest beach is thirty minutes away, there's plenty of hunting and fishing available, and the weather, despite the summer heat, also can be postcard perfect. It's a great place to raise a family, and I still call it home.

My parents, Jackie and David Ross, were my first role models. Much of how I act and think has to do with my parents and the examples they set. When I saw my mom and dad get up and go to work every day, at the crack of dawn, I understood the importance of hard work and commitment. My dad was one of those guys who believed you needed to be on time. In fact, if you were on time, you were late. Dad spent three years in the navy as a cook, and he believed in those values and has followed them to this day. You showed up for work on time, you worked hard, and you did what you were supposed to do. And repeat it all the next day.

I also learned the importance of humility from them—and to be grateful for what you have. I am the middle child, sandwiched between my older sister, Shannon, and younger sister, Nikki. When my parents married in 1974, they lived in a two-bedroom, one-bathroom home on the south side of town. It was a low-income area, and I bet that house was less than one thousand square feet. My parents eventually enclosed the carport and made it into the master bedroom. Neither one of my parents attended college, but they worked really hard and provided for their kids. That is how I learned to appreciate the value of a dollar.

Dad worked for Livingston Provision Company, a business that processed and delivered meats to area restaurants and schools. He arrived each day to work at 4 a.m. I spent several summers crawling around in those freezers, helping make deliveries and earning one hundred dollars a week—and thinking I was rich. Dad officially retired in 2007 but still works part-time for the same company. Mom worked for the Florida State University athletic department in ticket sales. She later was in charge of ticket sales at the Donald L. Tucker Civic Center and also worked for the Department of Highway Safety before she retired in 2014. On top of that, she was a full-time mom.

Every penny counted in our home. That's why technically I am not a Tallahassee native, though I have lived there my entire life with the exception of my first thirty-six hours or so. My parents saved $1,500 dollars when I was born on March 19, 1977—in Bainbridge, Georgia. The delivery cost at the Tallahassee hospital was $1,700 compared to $200 at the Bainbridge hospital, so they packed up and headed north on the day I was born.

Suffice to say the phrase "humble beginnings" applies! And as an adult, baseball would continue to keep me humble.

◇

Time for a confession: Although I played fifteen years in the big leagues (2002–16) with seven different organizations, played in 883 games, and am blessed with two World Series rings (with both the Boston Red Sox and the Cubs), I was never a big baseball fan growing up. I hardly ever watched baseball. It was boring. I'd much rather turn the TV to a game show or a basketball game. Those involved constant action. My childhood buddy Jason Jackson, still my best friend to this day, and I watched a game show called *Supermarket Sweep*. It was a show where contestants tried to win a timed shopping spree in a supermarket. Now that was fun, watching people dash around a grocery store, tossing products wildly into their carts.

Other friends of mine were baseball guys and knew all the players on every major-league team. I couldn't name half of them. That really didn't matter to me. But here's the thing: I loved *playing* the game. What I lacked as a fan, I made up for on the field.

I started out as a second baseman in youth baseball, but I soon discovered I loved to catch. I wanted to be in every play and I took pride in it. My future high school coach, Jeff Hogan, was the person who suggested to my father that I move to catcher. Second basemen were a dime a dozen, he said. Being the guy behind the plate was never boring.

I played on the fields at Capital and Winthrop parks in Tallahassee's youth league and, back in the day, was known as a power hitter—this from a guy who only hit 106 home runs in the big leagues! I may have been chubby as a young kid, but I had some pop in my bat. Plus, I also loved playing defense, throwing runners out and getting into all that catcher equipment. I was confident in my abilities, even then. I just always believed in myself.

That carried over into high school at Florida High, which at that time was located on the Florida State University campus, near downtown. Our baseball program under Coach Jeff Hogan was a perennial contender for the state title. I learned a lot from Coach Hogan and carried those lessons with me into the majors. I was always a good bunter and that was a skill coach Hogan taught and emphasized to every player. Coach Hogan fostered a good atmosphere on the team, where talented older players helped teach the younger guys how to play the game right. And when Coach Hogan retired, his assistant coach, John Hollenbeck, stepped in and continued to build the program's tradition.

During my freshman year, our starting catcher, Derek Reams—he later signed with FSU and played in the minor leagues for two years—couldn't play in a spring tournament game. I was thrown into the fire. I caught a senior pitcher and, if memory serves, we won the game 1–0. My approach didn't change, whatever the circumstances. I just tried to focus and concentrate on the moment and not be overwhelmed. I wasn't the best player on the team by any means, but I was confident. I wasn't afraid to speak up, either. If somebody had a bad attitude in the dugout—no matter if he was a freshman or an upperclassman—I wasn't afraid to say something. I was willing to do whatever it took to win that day. I was focused on the moment. I didn't care about how I looked because it wasn't about me.

Even in high school, I enjoyed the management aspects of being a catcher. I was always observing what was happening with our pitcher and the other team's batters. I enjoyed talking to the coaches and my teammates, saying things like, "Hey, we're not getting this pitch today, so let's stay away from it." Or "We can't throw this pitch anymore to that guy." The coaches would sit down with me and ask, "Hey, what are you seeing today?" I took that part of the game much more seriously than I did my offense. I was never the player who took a million swings in the batting cage. And I guess it showed in my average. But I loved to catch, read the hitters, throw out base runners, and work with the pitchers to get them through the game. Even in high school I loved managing the ups and downs of the game. I am as competitive as anyone—I was tossed from one high school game for arguing balls and strikes—but I also felt it was my responsibility to keep a teammate from boiling over. If everyone else was losing their head, I needed to keep mine on.

Baseball was my game, but I loved basketball, too. It was my favorite sport. I played hoops at Florida High for Al Blizzard. But since my potential was in baseball, Blizzard asked me to promise I'd commit to basketball for the three years after I made the varsity team as a sophomore. Blizzard didn't want me taking a roster spot from another player who really wanted to play if I planned to quit after one season. Quit? There wasn't a three-point shot I'd pass up. You have to shoot to score, right? Once it was clear my future was baseball, however—I was being recruited by many of the country's top college baseball programs by my senior year in 1995—Coach

Blizzard told me it was okay for me to quit basketball to concentrate on baseball, if that's what I wanted.

I told him I loved basketball and made a commitment to play all three years, and that's what I did. And I enjoyed every minute of it.

. . . .

DAVID'S iPHONE JOURNAL
2/8/16

Had a chance to go hang with a buddy this last weekend for a super bowl party. My wife and I went to Auburn to spend the weekend with Tim and Kim Hudson. Tim and I played together at Auburn and in Atlanta. He is a guy I have thought of as a great friend and mentor. Tim just finished his last year of a 17 year career with the SF Giants. It was nice to get his perspective on his last year and the things he tried to do. He talked a lot about the things that are becoming more important to me the longer I'm in this game, and that is the relationships. We talked about a lot of special people we have been able to play with and how they made us better players and people. How the bond you create will never go away even long after baseball, that's what I am most proud of. He also talked about trying to compete when the tank is empty, that's what I'm most scared of!!! No one enjoys failing, especially when you feel like you are letting down the guys

you care most about. I don't want to embarrass
myself. Anyways, it was a great weekend with
the Hudson family and just made me even more
excited about the journey of this season.

· · · · · · · · · · · · · · · ·

I always tried to take everything in stride, even during my college recruitment. I had shoe boxes and shoe boxes of letters from colleges around the country, and I had made official visits to Auburn, Miami, Tulane, North Carolina State, and Tennessee. FSU was in my backyard and recruited me as well—I peddled soft drinks in FSU's baseball stadium as a kid—so I had the pick of some of the best baseball programs in the country.

My dad has always had a great and very dry sense of humor. In high school I'd tell him I was leaving the house at 8:45 p.m. for a 9 p.m. movie, and he'd say, *okay, be back at 9:15 p.m.* One night Jason Jackson and I went out and before we left Dad gave me his standard *be back at 9:15 p.m.*—and then he surprised me by asking if I had made a decision on college yet. I told him I'd think about it the next day. I'd kept putting the decision off. Dad said, "No, I think you need to start really narrowing this thing down. People are waiting on you." He was right. So I made the decision on the spot. I told Dad, "All right, I'll go to Auburn," just like that, in the snap of a finger. Then Jason and I jumped in the car and went to the movies. FSU fans often wondered why I didn't attend FSU, but I felt I needed to get out of town and learn to live on my own. I never washed my own clothes or cooked a meal until I went to college.

I had been drafted in the nineteenth round of the 1995 Major League Amateur Draft by the Los Angeles Dodgers out of Florida High, but I had decided to go the college route instead. I played at Auburn in 1996–97. That's when I created my work ethic under Coach Hal Baird that carried into my professional career.

I think players have a mental choice to be either negative or positive in any given situation. Actually, we all have a choice of what we want our attitude to be. The longer I was in baseball, the more I knew one thing about the game: Nobody was going to feel sorry for you. The game moves on and you have to keep working and pushing forward to keep up.

My sophomore year in 1997, we played the NCAA regional tournament in my hometown of Tallahassee, at FSU. Talk about a cool moment. Beyond the left-field fence of the baseball stadium was my alma mater, Florida High. In our game against FSU, I started at catcher only because Casey Dunn had suffered a broken hand in the regional opener against South Carolina. We trailed 7–1 after six innings but managed to close the gap to 7–5 in the bottom of the ninth. I came to the plate with two runners on and immediately fell behind in the count 0–2. After taking a ball, I barely foul-tipped the next pitch. In fact, FSU players had already started to charge out of their dugout, thinking they won the game. Two pitches later, I hit a game-winning home run over the left-field fence. It was crazy. I was just trying to find my way and the next thing you know, I hit maybe one of the biggest home runs in school history.

We went on to win the regional tourney and advanced to the College World Series, where we lost to Stanford twice in the double-elimination bracket. We had a talented team, with guys like Tim Hudson, who pitched and played center field and is now one of my closest friends. He and I reunited in the big leagues with the Atlanta Braves from 2009 to 2012.

With Dunn healthy and returning—and after being asked to move to left field from catcher—I left Auburn on good terms and transferred to Florida for the 1998 season. Even though I was the new guy, I felt at home and immediately connected with the guys and Coach Andy Lopez. Again, it was about fitting into a new situation and being myself, on and off the field. Coach had enough confidence in me behind the plate that I was one of five or six catchers during his thirty-plus-year career allowed to call their own game. That experience helped me throughout my career in terms of understanding the strengths and weaknesses of pitching staffs and opposing hitters. Gators pitcher Josh Fogg also said I was the master of the "two-minute conversation" when I arrived. That was my way of making sure I introduced myself to everyone and letting them know I was going to work to be the best player I could be for the Florida Gators and do whatever it takes to win. And we did it together. Coach Lopez liked to say the ponies got all the attention, but it was the mules that helped make teams successful. It was a fun, talented team with guys like Fogg, Brad Wilkerson, and Mark Ellis. We made it to the College World Series that season as the number-one seed but lost our first two games to Mississippi State and Southern California.

When I reflect back on it, it's clear to me how fortunate I was during that time of my development, from youth baseball to high school to college. In addition to those teams, I had the chance to travel the country with the 18U Team USA Baseball team and played in the Junior Olympics. I never had any expectations when it came to making any of those teams. I really just enjoyed competing and playing and being part of a big group. I think I've always had that quality in me. Do I always want to play? Yes. Just keep doing your thing, just keep working hard.

Following my junior season at Florida, I was drafted again by the Los Angeles Dodgers, this time in the seventh round of the 1998 amateur draft.

Another journey was set to begin.

CHAPTER 2

TIME FOR A NAP

1 P.M.

Baseball is a game of routines, and, whenever we had night games on the road, my routine included afternoon naps. A midday snooze always seemed to give me a fresh start. But, of course, Game Seven of the World Series was neither an ordinary night game nor an ordinary road game. Thinking it would help my focus, I tried my best to treat that final day like it was any other, but it was nearly impossible.

It was also a hectic morning. Cole still wasn't feeling well and his chest was tight, so Hyla grabbed a cab and rode around downtown Cleveland in search of an open pharmacy. By late morning, Cole started to feel a little better. That allowed us to relax—and for me to take a sixty-minute booster nap!

The first of two Cubs team buses to Progressive Field was scheduled for 3:30 p.m. The early bus is usually crowded, and my nerves were starting to kick in again. Hoping it would calm them, I decided to walk the six blocks to the field. I thought it would help me relax and enjoy the moment. It was a comfortable afternoon with temps in the mid-sixties and overcast skies.

I got dressed and was ready to walk out the door of our hotel suite when I turned to give Hyla a good-bye hug. My wife has been my rock throughout my professional baseball journey. I was always the emotional one; she was always calm, cool, and collected. In fact, if Hyla gets emotional about anything, good or bad, she gets even more reserved and keeps those feelings to herself.

This time the roles were reversed, and it caught me completely off guard. I looked at Hyla, and her green eyes gave away her thoughts.

She was crying.

. . . .

DAVID'S iPHONE JOURNAL
2/15/16

Nerves are starting to kick in!! It's Monday night and I'm flying out Wednesday. Feel like this off season has flown by. Got my last three work outs in and trying to hug my wife and kids as much as possible! Not sure if as an adult I give my kids enough credit for knowing what's going on. They have asked me at least 10 times this month when I'm leaving. It must be on their brain much more than I thought. My daughter has started sleeping in the shirt I got her for when I leave and my son is glued to my hip. I think he is going to have the toughest time. I'm really excited to get out to AZ with the boys but I have the biggest pit in my stomach about leaving. All of these feelings, and the fact that it is really tough getting my body where it needs to be, are all signs that help me realize I am ready for this to be the last year.

. . . .

Meeting Hyla turned out to be one of my life's great blessings. And, for the record, she called first and asked me out, though she likes to say otherwise.

I was a junior at Florida High in 1994 and Hyla was a sophomore at nearby Godby High. Hyla's older brother Jason had transferred to my school from Godby and was playing baseball as a senior. Hyla and her younger sister attended our games to watch Jason, who initially wasn't keen on his sisters hanging around the team. Even during our spring tournament when everyone was at the hotel pool between games, Jason wanted his sisters to keep their distance. But we all had mutual friends, and Hyla and I got to be friends. One day Hyla called and said she wanted my help to set up a double date—her best friend with my best friend. Hyla and I were supposed to keep them company.

Half of the plan worked out perfectly. Hyla and I started to date.

Even then Hyla was a straight shooter, and said exactly what was on her mind. I thought I was a bigwig on the Florida High campus, the star baseball player being recruited by the best college teams. My mom was the type whose love means she'll do anything for her kids, and she did everything for her son. If I wanted something to eat, Mom cooked it. If I wanted something to drink, Mom got it. Hyla marched to a different drummer. While at her house when we first started to date, Hyla asked me if I wanted something to drink.

I said, "Please, thanks. I will take a sweat tea." Hyla pointed toward the kitchen and said, "It's in the fridge, you can get it yourself." I knew immediately she was a keeper.

I signed to play baseball at Auburn University and Hyla attended Auburn a year later. But the out-of-state tuition was too expensive, and she returned home to Tallahassee and transferred to Florida State. Hyla earned a degree in nursing and became a pediatric ICU nurse. For my part, I moved from Auburn to Florida and then, in 1998, was drafted by the Los Angeles Dodgers in June. Hyla and I dated off and on in college, at one point taking nearly a two-year stretch off.

We were busy with life, but even so, Hyla and I never lost communication with each other. Truthfully, I really missed her. In 2001, while I was with the Jacksonville (Florida) Suns, the Dodgers' Double-A affiliate, she showed up unannounced at one of our home games. Before she left for the game, Hyla's mother had asked her, "Honey, what if he has a girlfriend in the stands?" Hyla smiled and said it would be a quick trip in that case. It turned out to be the trip of a lifetime. I was so happy to see Hyla that we got back together, this time for good.

Nurses can have flexibility in their jobs, and Hyla was able to relocate to Jacksonville in the summer of 2001 and took a job at Wolfson Children's Hospital. Though we also got engaged that year—I popped the question during a dolphin swim at Discovery Cove in Orlando—she wasn't thrilled about living the "baseball life," which can be unpredictable, especially for minor-league players.

Jacksonville in 2001 was already the fifth team I had played for in four years, all within the Dodgers' minor-league organization. Stops included Yakima, Washington; Vero Beach, Florida; San

Bernardino, California; San Antonio, Texas; and Jacksonville, Florida. Hyla's plan was to wait for me to be done with baseball before we were married. She really enjoyed her work as a nurse and felt she would give up a part of herself if she followed me around in baseball. I was never a prospect or a star in the Dodgers' organization, so we figured I'd play for another year or two and then move on to another career. That is why our engagement went into extra innings—as in four years.

I loved baseball and always thought it would be a part of my life, but I was realistic. Playing in the major leagues was never a goal. Many of my teammates over the years were in the game one day, out the next. That's how the game works. Every June, more than one thousand draft-eligible players are selected in Major League Baseball's amateur draft. That doesn't include the hundreds signed as free agents.

When I played at Triple-A Las Vegas in 2002, Hyla remained in Jacksonville and worked, visiting Las Vegas when time allowed. When I was called up by the Dodgers and made my big-league debut on June 29, 2002, at age twenty-five against the Anaheim Angels—I pinch-hit for Shawn Green in the top of the ninth inning and struck out swinging against reliever Aaron Sele—Hyla wasn't able to attend. (She did make it to St. Louis seven days later on July 6 for my first career start, a 4–2 win over the Cardinals.)

Hyla wanted me to succeed in baseball and for us to be married, but she didn't want to be married to baseball. Her parents were divorced and she didn't want to go down that path, either. Hyla had worked too hard to become a nurse and her career was important. In Hyla's heart, she wanted us to be together full-time when we were married. In the meantime, she was patient enough to wait out the uncertainty surrounding my baseball career.

Now that I'd made it to the big leagues, however, the calculus had started to change. It was during a visit to Los Angeles late in the 2004 regular season that Hyla had a change of heart. She sat in the stands with the wife of one of our coaches—Hyla admired and respected this woman—and they talked about "baseball life" and "real life." The woman asked Hyla, "What are you doing?" Hyla responded, "What do you mean?" Hyla explained she enjoyed being a nurse and wasn't interested in getting caught up in baseball life. Hyla admitted she was fighting against that lifestyle of following me from city to city. The woman asked Hyla if she loved me, and explained how a player's career in professional baseball can end at any time. She encouraged Hyla to enjoy the baseball journey, as well as her career in nursing. The message hit home because we were married that off-season in St. Petersburg, Florida, in 2005.

. . . .

DAVID'S iPHONE JOURNAL
2/16/16

Night before I leave and laying down with my kids. So sick to my stomach about leaving my family tomorrow. Can tell my wife is anxious, and kids just started balling after dinner. Landri wants more time and Cole keeps telling me he is going to cry his head off in the morning. I have tried to just let the day go as normal but they keep bringing it up. I'm afraid that I'm going to have one of those ugly, trying to hold back tears, cry faces while dropping

them off at school in the morning. I know it will all
be fine once everyone settles into the new routine
but that is not helping the sick feeling I have. So
many things will have changed next time I see
them Harper will look like she has aged two years! I
know I'm not a perfect dad but knowing how much
they will miss me makes me feel like I'm doing
something right. I love these guys!

• • • • • • • • • • • • • • • • • •

Hyla is a wonderful mom, and one of the strongest women I
know.

We've enjoyed a good life, but like every family we've had bumps
in the road. One of the scariest was when Hyla had our youngest
daughter, Harper, on August 26, 2015. I didn't know if either my
wife or daughter would survive. Hyla was rushed to a Tallahassee hospital for an emergency cesarean section, two months ahead
of her scheduled due date. Hyla had suffered a partial abruption,
which is an uncommon yet serious complication of pregnancy in
which the placenta separates from the uterus.

We were in the middle of my first season with the Cubs, and
I rushed back from Chicago to be by her side. I was an emotional
wreck by the time I arrived from Chicago. Doctors explained Hyla
could have bled to death, and Harper could have died due to a lack
of oxygen. Thankfully, the emergency C-section was a success.
When Harper was born she weighed a mere 3 pounds, 11 ounces
and was 17 inches long. She had to stay in the neonatal intensive
care unit for the next month, but by the time she left the hospital,
she was as healthy and happy a baby as you could hope for.

That wasn't my family's only trip to the emergency room. In March 2014, while I was in spring training in Fort Myers, Florida, with the Boston Red Sox, my son Cole experienced trouble breathing and his mouth was turning blue. He ended up being fine, but the scary incident revealed that he suffers from asthma and that he would need medication and an inhaler. Again, Hyla was strong as a rock, while I was an emotional mess.

Hyla never gets too high or too low, and she can keep "baseball life" and "real life" in perspective. Me? Not so much. My emotions can be on full display, on and off the field.

Hyla always knows how to keep me in the right perspective, too. I can still remember it clear as day. In August 2006, when I was with the Cincinnati Reds, I hit a game-winning, two-run home run in the tenth inning to beat the first-place St. Louis Cardinals 8–7. There's nothing better than a walk-off home run, and I was on cloud nine. I hit a 442-foot home run off Cardinals reliever Jason Isringhausen that landed on the roof of the batter's eye beyond the center-field fence. It was a big win for us because we were still battling with the Cardinals in the National League Central division. We had just had our daughter Landri, so Hyla did not attend the game, and I couldn't wait to get home to tell Hyla all about my heroics. I walked in the door and Landri was still up, screaming because she had an inner ear infection.

Hyla said, "Here, take her and try to be a dad. I know you're a hero, but I need a break."

◇

On the afternoon of Game Seven, I gave Hyla a "What's wrong look?" as we stood at the door of our suite. I was ready to head to Progressive Field but Hyla, my rock, had started to cry. As I tried to focus on the game, the emotion of our journey together in professional baseball had bubbled to the surface. She didn't know why it had hit her at that moment, but it did. I laughed, only because, for once, the roles were reversed. Hyla was thinking about me and how my career was coming to an end. I was more stressed about the game and retirement was the furthest thought from my mind. We hugged and she shooed me out the door.

I stopped at the Starbucks in the hotel lobby for one last iced coffee. I get a Starbucks coffee in the morning and a Starbucks iced coffee in the afternoon. Like I said, I'm a man of routine. I tell Hyla it makes me a better dad. I need the energy for when the kids get home from school. As I started toward Progressive Field, my coffee in hand, I put my headphones in and turned up the country music group Old Dominion.

About halfway to the stadium, I bumped into baseball writer Jon Heyman. We walked together and chitchatted about baseball life. Jon asked me about what I planned to do after baseball, but I didn't say much. I thought to myself, I don't care what I am doing after baseball. We've got Game Seven in a few hours. When I reached the stadium and our locker room, I made sure to greet everybody, a ritual I started early in my career. It was around 4 p.m. and plenty of guys already were in the locker room. Dexter Fowler, Anthony Rizzo, and Tommy La Stella were playing the video game Mario Kart. They were the everyday players when it came to Mario Kart and they really got after it, too. Part of me said, All right, they are nice and relaxed. Another part of me said, Hey, we've got the World Series tonight.

As soon as the guys saw me, many of them started to make it about me. Outfielder Matt Szczur asked how I felt, was I excited: "Hey, it's your last game." I appreciated it but I told Matt and the others I was fine, that I was really just focused on winning. There was so much emotion surrounding this game, but I tried to be completely unemotional when it was about me. Game Seven was the last game of my career but it was the furthest thing from my mind as I sat in front of my locker and got dressed.

Still, I knew I would be pissed for the rest of my life if we lost this game.

CHAPTER 3

BALL BAGS

5 P.M.

The pregame stretch is usually just for the guys in the starting lineup that day. On the day of Game Seven, Tim Buss, the strength and conditioning coach for the Chicago Cubs since 2001, led the exercises. Buss is one of the best in the biz. He always knows how to get the most out of the guys, how to motivate them and keep everyone loose and lively. I wasn't in the starting lineup but knew there was a good chance I'd play that night. That was my focus. Plus, I wanted to be out there in pregame stretch with the guys.

Buss is also the de facto team psychologist and motivator. During the 2016 spring training, he developed a team ritual that he termed "Ball Bags." It consisted of a simple but an effective conversation that only took a few minutes. Players gathered in a circle before the start of the pregame stretch and Tim proceeded to share funny scenarios or embarrassing things that happened to players that day or that week. He gathered stories from what he heard players say, like "You won't believe what so-and-so did in the clubhouse a few days ago."

"Bussy" dished it out and often made fun of a player or a coach to lighten the mood. In spring training, some of our relievers got their revenge when they tied Buss up and strapped him to a chair for warm-ups. He is a master at helping to build team chemistry.

While the ritual slowed once the regular season got into full swing, Buss still gathered players together before pregame stretch when he felt we needed a pick-me-up. For instance, he might single out one player—take Kris Bryant—and demand that we go around in the circle and say something nice about him. Buss would yell, "Go!" and then, one by one, we went around the circle and everyone shared comments such as "Oh, he's got beautiful eyes." "He's the best baseball player I've ever seen." Or "His girlfriend's hot." Utility infielder Munenori Kawasaki spoke in Japanese. That didn't stop Buss. He would "interpret" Kawasaki's remarks as he saw fit, which was hilarious. The idea was to have fun with it, and players clapped and cheered for every comment.

During the playoffs, which began with the National League Division Series against the San Francisco Giants, Buss made sure we met before every playoff game. All seventeen of them, as it turned out. On some days the comments were more serious, but it was always a great way to help players relax. When Jon Lester started the NLDS opener against San Francisco on Friday, October 7, 2016, I was in the lineup and Buss asked the players to say some nice things about me. It probably won't surprise you to learn that more than a few wisecracks were made about my age.

While I wasn't in the starting lineup for Game Seven in Cleveland, I headed over to the batting cage where the guys were assembling for the pregame stretch. I wanted to be a part of it one final time. I wanted to enjoy the moment, but I also wanted to let the guys know I was fully invested in this game, too. I knew there was a chance I would play if Lester, as planned, was used in relief. When we gathered in a circle, Buss surprised me when he pointed my way and asked the guys to say something nice about me.

I was left holding the bag, so to speak.

. . . .

DAVID'S iPHONE JOURNAL
2/19/16

Wow, what a great feeling walking back into the locker room and seeing all your buddies! It's such a great feeling to be laughing and joking with the boys again, can't believe it's starting back! The weather is perfect and there is a great vibe around the team. Had a chance to golf with Lester, [John] Lackey, and [Eric] Hinske yesterday at Estancia, one of the nicest courses I have ever played. You forget how much you love these guys until you get back around them. Looking forward to getting going tomorrow and starting this journey.

. . . .

Are you sure you want to retire?

I was asked that question a bunch in 2016. The best part was the fact I, as a backup catcher, went out on my own terms. That is a luxury not afforded to every player. Major League Baseball is invitation-only, and players are usually told when to leave. I look back and I am so thankful I got to go out the way I wanted. I played professional baseball twenty-one years, including six seasons in the minors. I made more money than I could have ever imagined, won two World Series, and met so many people who have influenced my life and will be lifelong friends.

Heck, I thought my career might have ended when I was released by the Cincinnati Reds on August 19, 2008. But it proved to be the best thing that happened to me professionally and personally. I also thought my career might have ended when I missed sixty games with a concussion in 2013 with the Boston Red Sox. That was a dark, scary time, but I returned with the help of so many amazing, supportive people, including my family, and won my first World Series ring. In the end, I think everything happens for a reason.

Baseball is a metaphor for life, and I grinded every day. I didn't have any other choice. I was a head-down, task-oriented player. I told my teammates all the time that I didn't have the talent or the luxury to look ahead. I had to focus on today, not tomorrow. I had to give 100 percent every day. If I was still with the team tomorrow, I'd give 100 percent then, too. I had to stay involved and invested in the moment. I also was the product of a lot of great people who helped me along the way, so they deserve credit in my development as a person, player, and a teammate, too. I look back on my life and think how I even got fifteen years in the major leagues and it blows my mind. I tried not to take anything for granted.

Could I have played another year? Yes. I could have made a bunch more money. I joked with Jed Hoyer, executive vice president and general manager, to make me a qualifying offer, a one-year contract that is the average of the top 125 salaries in baseball, which was $17.2 million in 2016. I would have signed on the dotted line and stayed in a heartbeat. I'm not stupid.

My skills had not diminished as much as I thought in 2016 either. My 10 home runs and 32 RBI, for instance, were my best marks since 2007, when I hit 17 home runs with 39 RBI with Cincinnati. I thought I contributed defensively, managed the game, and helped us win. I loved baseball, don't get me wrong. I loved competing. I loved my teammates. And Chicago was the perfect atmosphere because of what president of baseball operations Theo Epstein, General Manager Hoyer, and Manager Joe Maddon created. I just felt it was time to go home to Tallahassee. I wanted to start a different chapter in my life and enjoy my family.

I always liked the story my former Reds teammate Scott Hatteberg told me about the three types of guys who go to a party. There's that guy who leaves the party early and doesn't have as good a time as he'd like. There's that guy who stays just the right amount of time and leaves when he knows it's time, when everybody starts to wind down. Then there's that last guy at the party, the one who's too drunk and won't go home. You've probably met that guy at some point, or been him. I didn't want to be that last guy, the annoying one who just hangs around and is asked to leave. I understood that when a player retired, you are gone and forgotten pretty fast, especially a guy like me. It was a crazy ride and I am humbled by everything that has happened, and continues to happen, to me and my family because of baseball.

◇

The idea of being a good teammate gets thrown around a lot. And I think a lot of players take it seriously. But what does it really mean?

There are many components to being a good teammate, and many players do some of those things well. It includes simple things like showing up on time because that means you are reliable and the next guy can count on you. Another component is always being prepared. That allows the people around you to know that you will get your job done and they can rely on you. Being supportive is another big one. Maybe the guy next to you in the locker room is struggling and needs your help. That can be part of being a good teammate.

I think good teammates have a high level of self-awareness. If you are self-aware, you have a better chance of focusing on the moment, you have a better chance of processing information. If you know yourself and are able to make adjustments, you will improve as a player, or have the potential to help those around you improve, because you understand them. Self-awareness is tied to authenticity. People who lack self-awareness tend to be more narcissistic because they can't truly read themselves.

During my two years with the Cubs, I felt like I had a good feel for the clubhouse and was able to share my feelings with humility. Humility helped me connect with people. I never claimed to know more than the next guy. With help from my teammates, I think we created a season-long dialogue in the clubhouse about baseball. Everyone was receptive and approachable, and that was important. We grew closer and that helped us work together over the course of a six-month season.

What's going on in a given player's head is always different than the next guy. To be a good teammate, you have to be focused on the moment—not the other dramas playing out in your head. Too many players nowadays don't sit on the bench and watch the game. I watched every game and I was invested in my teammates' at-bats and what they did defensively. I could tell when a teammate wasn't into that game or maybe he was just dragging that day. Maybe he just had a rough day or he was tired. I tried to pay attention to my teammates, whether they had good or bad at-bats, whether they took their bats to the field, whether other problems popped up. If I didn't pay attention, I wouldn't have been able to help.

Whether I was scheduled to play on a given day or not, I always tried to bring my personality and my energy to the ballpark. That was a very important part of being a good teammate to me. If I didn't have my energy that day, it was difficult to invest in the team. If I was dragging or not into it that day, I hurt the team. (Now you know why I need that Starbucks on the way to the field.) And my teammates expected it of me. As a veteran, if I was not checked in at all times, it took away from my credibility. It would be hard to criticize a teammate and be respected. I think that's important from a manager and as a professional baseball player—you've got to be the same guy every day. Everyone has good and bad days and mood swings. I did, too. But I tried to be the same guy every day that I went to the field.

I always tried to engage people. In 2015, shortstop Addison Russell was called up to the twenty-five-man roster on April 21, 2015. He was a real quiet, reserved guy. I don't mind that. But I talked to him all the time. There were times he'd walk right past me and not say hello. I was, "Hey man, it doesn't take a whole lot of effort for you to say hello to me. Don't walk by me again and not say hello." That was my way of being a veteran and getting on a rookie. I said the same thing to third baseman Kris Bryant. "Just say hello to me, we're teammates." I just wanted to engage with him for a few seconds—even if I couldn't understand how he spelled his first name. In spring training of 2015 I called him "CB" for the first week. And one day he finally worked up the nerve to come to me and let me know that *Kris* was spelled with a *K*. Lesson learned. Learn how to spell the superstar's name!

I didn't want to walk the hallways and not say hello to some-body. I didn't go looking for people, but I had a routine. I walked in and said hello to the trainers, to the strength coaches. I walked into our locker room and said hello to anyone in there at the time. When our bullpen catcher, Chad Noble, arrived, he'd shake my hand and say, "Good morning, sir," or "Good afternoon, sir." He said "sir" to me every time and it was a good laugh. It was a bright spot to start my workday.

I had an edge, too, which probably helped me play as long as I did. As a player and a team, you have to be fearless. I tried to bring that quality to the locker room, too. If I criticized a player, I wanted to do it in a way that it was a teaching moment. I had made my share of mistakes, and the key was to learn from those mistakes. Our manager, Joe Maddon, said I did things that maybe 5 or 10 per-cent of the guys he had been around were capable of doing daily. He called me "unique." In my career, I encountered some guys who are just there for themselves. I tried to be there for everybody else and not make it all about me.

My belief in engaging people goes beyond a clubhouse. The more you get to know people, the better you can cope with issues that crop up along the way. That can come in handy in sports or in the workplace. When you know your teammates, you know how to talk to them. Take pitchers, for example. There were some pitchers during my career I had to push to their complete max because they didn't know how to push themselves. They needed somebody else to do it. There were guys I had to sweet-talk all the time because they were so negative in their thought process. "Oh, that was a crappy pitch. Oh, what am I doing wrong?" My approach was turn the page, stay positive. There are times, as a pitcher, when you make the perfect pitch and it's smacked into the gap.

I had to know my teammates and their personalities because when that crucial time arrived in the middle of the game, I was the one who had to go out there and talk to them. Catchers have to be psychologists with their pitchers. You have to know when to yell and scream, or explain something, or pat them on the butt. But they trusted me because I got to know them and I was invested in them. In the heat of the battle, I learned how to talk to that particular pitcher and get the most out of him in those tough situations.

I wanted to do well, too, but I never thought of myself as a selfish player. I took pride in my craft and I wanted to do well because I didn't want to be embarrassed or fail. I tried to put myself in a position to help make other players better. I always tried to be in the game, when I was playing or not. I wanted to study and hear everything that went on. If somebody said something I didn't agree with, I wanted to be among the first to discuss why they felt that way.

I didn't start off doing all those things to be a good teammate. I did all those things because I wanted to win. At times I got angry, too. Again, it was about being focused on the moment. One day I was on the field for pregame batting practice with the Cubs and Buss was rehabbing an injured player. I was in the cage taking my swings and Buss was at second base with the player, who was not in the game but was working on his leadoffs while our pitcher threw batting practice. Buss asked the pitcher if he could pause between throws to help the rehabbing player with his timing and rhythm. I lost it. I jumped from the cage and screamed at Tim, "We're not here for him! We're not here for him! He can't help us win tonight! This is about us! We are getting loose! You need to bring that guy out three hours earlier! This is not about him!" Buss could have easily told me, "Go shit in your hat, dude," but it was a teaching moment for all of us.

In the 2015 National League Division Series opener at St. Louis, Phil Cuzzi was the home plate umpire and he struggled with the strike zone. I started at catcher with Jon Lester on the mound for us, but both teams complained about Cuzzi. Our guys went from the dugout into the video room and everyone was angry. I was pissed with the guys complaining and bitching, so I turned and said, "Hey, he's not going to cost us the game. You just need to relax, focus on the W. Relax and get off the umpires. It's not him, it's us." We lost that game but ended up winning that series; it was a reminder that we had to focus on the things that were actually within our control.

Over the years I developed a philosophy about always being engaged, being part of a group, being positive, concentrating on the things within our control, and lifting guys up. Baseball is a negative game. It's a game of failure and, as players, you need to stay positive. If not, a long season gets longer. Winning was the ultimate goal and it was important for everyone to do their part. My part happened to involve bringing some energy and lifting guys up as much as I could. Sure, I was not that guy every day. On days when I was in the lineup, I was different, more on edge. I was more focused on my job those days. But, as a backup player, it also helped me over the course of the season in that role because I could spend more of my energy on the team than I did myself. Being a good teammate and leader, in the long run, wasn't about numbers. It was about presence and how you were perceived by the rest of the group. That's what mattered most. Talent is part of the equation, but when you combine talent with accountability and authenticity, it is tough to beat.

. . . .

DAVID'S iPHONE JOURNAL
2/20/16

First day is over! It's always fun after the first day
is over because you get a gauge of how you feel.
Was fun to squat again, caught Lester and [Justin]
Grimm. Skip gave a great talk about expectations
and pressure. He wants us to focus on the daily
process. That's exactly how it was on the '13 Red
Sox. You just came every day and gave your best,
win or lose, you came back and did it again the
next day. The stretch today had a great feeling
about it, music was blaring and everyone was
smiling. It's funny listening to the new guys talk
about how great it is here, I was thinking the same
thing last year. I can't wait for the position players
to all get here, feels like it's going to be a great
camp.

. . . .

On the field, as we gathered in our circle before pregame stretch
in Game Seven against the Indians, everyone was excited, clapping
and yelling. Buss started his spiel and he pointed at me. "Okay,
everyone say something nice about David Ross. Go!" I tried to not

get emotional but it was difficult. Some of the players got emotional, too. I had my own personal anxiety because I knew there was a good chance I'd play in the middle innings. Rizzo was one of the first to speak, and he went into a routine about how "he's my dad, he takes care of me, I can't imagine what it's going to be like without him. I don't want him to think about it and I need to prepare for this game, but I owe everything that I got on this field to David Ross."

Outfielder Ben Zobrist is spiritual, and he talked about how certain people in his life were important to him; he talked about what I had done for the Cubs and for him as a person, and that he couldn't thank me enough. I was, he told everyone, by far the best teammate he's had. Outfielder Jason Heyward called me his brother and thanked me for helping him when he came up with the Atlanta Braves when we were both there. Second baseman Javier Baez talked about my red-ass and said I could be very angry. But he said I was honest and a great teammate. And Munenori Kawasaki, of course, spoke in Japanese, which allowed Buss to translate into I was an "average pickle with huge potatoes, huge balls."

In 2016, I was the last "Ball Bag" and that was fine with me.

CHAPTER 4

FIRST PITCH

8:02 P.M.

E very guy has a different routine for the hour before game time.

On the night of Game Seven, players like Kris Bryant and some others jumped in the cage to hit, but I skipped BP like I normally did. The locker room had a good vibe to it. Guys were doing their own thing, playing Mario Kart or getting something to eat. I am a nibbler before games so I wasn't hungry.

As I sat in front of my locker and got dressed in my game uniform, I allowed myself to reflect on the moment and realize how thankful I was. I really appreciated that World Series patch on the left sleeve. That doesn't come around very often. After I got dressed, I headed out to the field and down the right-field line to play catch with bullpen catcher Franklin Font. A sold-out crowd in excess of thirty-five thousand was expected at Progressive Field and at least half of the fans seemed to be rooting for the Cubs. I could already feel the energy and excitement of the crowd. I looked for my wife, Hyla, in the stands—Cubs families sat behind our dugout, near home plate—but I didn't see her. (I found out later Cole still wasn't feeling well so they hadn't made it to their seats.)

There was a calmness in the dugout before the game. There wasn't much rah-rah; everyone was excited and ready. Everyone seemed locked in. It was like, "Here we go, boys."

Dexter Fowler, take a bow.

Dexter, our leadoff hitter, opened Game Seven of the World Series with a solo home run off Cleveland's Corey Kluber in the top of the first inning.

The left-handed hitting Fowler, on the fourth pitch of the game off the right-handed Kluber, socked a sinker over the center-field fence and past the glove of a leaping Rajai Davis to give us a 1–0 lead. It was a historic swing: the first-ever leadoff home run in a Game Seven of the World Series.

Our dugout exploded. Everyone was jacked up by Fowler's blast. I was happy, too, but not jump-up-and-down happy. In fact, I'm not even sure I moved. I was expressionless on the outside, only because I was such a wreck inside. I didn't want to take the fun out of the moment, but my emotions were so high that I think I would've passed out if I cut loose. The past month had drained me emotionally, with everything that had gone on surrounding my last season and not knowing when it would all end.

In a way, however, it was probably better that I kept cool. I was eaten up in 2015, absolutely miserable after we fell just short of making it to the World Series. We'd fought our way back in 2016, rallying from a 3–1 deficit in the best-of-seven series, and now it was Game Seven. I was so wound up, stressed, and focused on winning that I didn't really react to Fowler's home run.

I remember looking over to the Cleveland dugout as Fowler rounded the bases. The home run took the wind out of the Indians and their fans. We knew we had to get an early lead against Kluber, especially with Indians reliever Andrew Miller fresh on three days' rest. Kluber had won the Cy Young Award in 2014, and was looking to become the first pitcher to win three starts in one World Series since Detroit's Mickey Lolich in 1968. For his part, Miller already had a league-record 29 strikeouts in 17 innings of pitching in the 2016 postseason.

Fowler's home run was a big moment. All season long, when we had established a lead early in the game, we'd been a tough team to beat.

◇

The 2016 World Series between us and the Cleveland Indians was the 112th edition of Major League Baseball's fall classic. And this one was linked to history like no other. The two teams had the distinction of having the longest World Series droughts in the big leagues when they entered the best-of-seven series. Cubs fans had long been conditioned to expect the worst through the decades of disappointment and near misses. The Cubs hadn't won the World Series since 1908 (the longest drought in American sports history), while the Indians hadn't notched a championship since 1948.

In my first year with the Cubs in 2015, we won 97 games and made it to the National League Championship Series, where we lost to the New York Mets. We entered the 2016 season as everyone's favorite to win the World Series and sweep aside the Curse of the Billy Goat, the black cat, and the memory of Steve Bartman. Our manager, Joe Maddon, repeatedly said he wouldn't hide from those expectations.

We followed Joe's lead, and it couldn't have gone any better. We were a young team—we entered the season with the third-youngest opening day roster in the major leagues behind the Houston Astros and the Milwaukee Brewers with an average age of 29.9, according to MLB.com. We had eight position players who were 26 years old or younger, including starters shortstop Addison Russell (22), outfielder Kyle Schwarber (23), third baseman Kris Bryant (24), first baseman Anthony Rizzo (26), and outfielder Jason Heyward (26). But we had the oldest starting rotation at 31.6 years and, of course, the backup catcher, yours truly, skewed the average with my thirty-nine years.

Turns out I wasn't the oldest player in the Major Leagues to open 2016. New York Mets starting pitcher Bartolo Colon, forty-two, had that honor, and was one of six forty-plus-year-olds on opening day rosters. I was one of four thirty-nine-year-olds. How about that? I had waited all my career to be in the top 10 of something!

You're only as old as you feel, right? And I felt good. The Cubs finished the regular season in 2016 with the best record in baseball at 103-58 and won our first National League Central title since 2008. We spent 180 days, including off days, in first place, won our division by seventeen and a half games, and never played under-.500 baseball. We reached the 100-win mark for the first time since 1935, and reached the World Series for the first time since 1945.

All the team's achievements in 2016 were especially poignant for me because I knew it was going to be my last season as a player. Following the 2015 season, I had made the decision that the next season, my fifteenth in the major leagues, would be my last. In November 2015 I was on MLB Network Radio on Sirius XM and I told the interviewer "it was time to be a dad." And it was. I played in 1,366 games—483 in the minors and 883 in the majors. I had worked hard, did the best I could, met some wonderful people, and had a lot of fun along the way.

Baseball afforded me a great life. But everyone measures success differently. Once you have the means to buy an expensive car, or buy everything else on your wish list, you still have to consider the things that money can't buy: love and happiness. If you are the kind of person who thinks counting dollars is the path to contentment, hell, you're never going to have enough. When is enough enough? If you call yourself a family man as I do, at some point you have to put your name and money where your mouth is.

Could I have played in 2017? Sure, I believe I could. In 2016, I was in the final season of a two-year, $5 million deal with the Cubs, and I probably could have made more money than I ever had in my career in 2017 with all the things that happened to me. But, you know what? Family matters more. And I always tried to put my family first.

Our 2016 Chicago Cubs team was a family, too. We were well aware of the Cubs' history and the long suffering of our fans. We listened to their stories and we were always thankful for their passion. We knew where they were coming from! But we also had to tune a little bit of that out because the 2016 season wasn't just about breaking a curse, or anything like that. If we started to get caught up in the nostalgia, it would've been impossible to do our job. That was what was great about our team. We never got caught up in history. It wasn't about the history. What I learned in Boston in 2013, when we won the World Series, is that you pulled into the stadium parking lot every day and did your job the best you could and to the best of your ability. I learned that if you started to look ahead or behind, you were in trouble.

Still, it was hard to keep the fans' excitement at bay. The main thing we heard about the stories from Cubs fans in 2016 was the tone of their voice, the nervousness and excitement. It was like a voice was constantly whispering in our ears, "They have to win the World Series." Well, that was our goal, to win the World Series, but we weren't focused on winning the World Series. We were focused on playing *today*. The more we won, the louder that voice grew.

Through it all, our team stayed really tight. A lot of credit for that is due to manager Joe Maddon. Joe doesn't have a whole lot of rules. I think that's the one thing that Joe has nailed and I think you will see other teams following suit. On other teams, the coach says "Okay, we've got early work today, we have this tomorrow, and so on." Joe wasn't like that at all. He didn't believe we needed to take batting practice every day. I believe batting practice is one of the most overrated things in baseball. (Maybe that's why I am a career .229 hitter!) The way Joe sees it, the last feeling you had at the plate is the one you want to take with you on your next at-bat. If you are hitting the ball well, why take more batting practice?

It's easy to slip into bad habits—or try too hard at the plate. I had my best year in Cincinnati (2006/.255 batting average, 21 home runs, and 52 RBIs) and I took the least amount of BP. I'd get in the cage and take a couple of swings to get loose and I'd be out of there. I was playing a lot—a career-high 112 games in 2007. Some days I had to fight through BP, when making all those adjustments might not actually help.

The brain is a powerful thing and sometimes it can work against you in baseball because you fail so often. The standard BP routine includes swinging for hits, bunts, hit-and-run, advancing the runner, and so on. With all those different scenarios, you begin manipulating your swing. For me, it was difficult enough just to hit the ball in a game when it's careening at you at 90 miles per hour. For me, obsessing about all those little adjustments didn't make sense, and Joe understood that. My strength was bunting, and Joe gave me the freedom to focus on that—the thing that mattered, in the heat of the game moment, was simply getting that runner to second or third base. Joe focused on your strengths and not your weaknesses.

Joe's laid-back approach didn't just eliminate needless practice. It also helped create a wonderful culture in the clubhouse that enabled players to enjoy their jobs and strive for success. Joe allowed you to be yourself as long as it didn't hinder others. He gave us complete and total freedom to be ourselves but we had to do it in a way that respected your teammates and respected the game. One of Joe's favorite sayings was "Respect ninety." That meant every time you hit the ball, you were going to bust your tail the ninety feet from home plate to first base. As a manager, Joe stayed out of the Cubs' locker room. He loathed meetings. He gave us, as players and as adults, the freedom to be ourselves. He allowed us to grow without getting in our way. Joe's belief was he only interfered if it was absolutely necessary.

In spring training in 2016, Joe met with the veterans (known as the lead bulls) and we discussed team policies, from dress code to who we wanted to allow in and out of the clubhouse. Joe said it didn't matter to him; he had his own office. He sat in first class on our charter flights, he was married, he didn't have kids who traveled with him, so he thought, Why would I want to make up a bunch of rules that I don't really need, that wouldn't really necessarily apply to me anyway? Joe told us to tell him what we wanted. And when that was done, he wanted to make sure we understood that we, as players, enforced them. Not him. So, when new players arrived in our locker room, regardless of their personality, it was our responsibility to make sure they understood everyone was held accountable. That there was right and there was wrong. So it was that player's responsibility to choose the right way. Joe felt that the greater freedom he gave the locker room, the greater respect and discipline management received in return.

My faith has also played in this process. I think when you have faith in God and a higher being, you are held accountable. It gives you that sense of I am accountable to somebody that is greater and it is a solid foundation when things go awry. At the end of the day, I am trying to be the best I can be and that's a hard enough job. To do what I think is the right thing by my faith and to be sure I am being the best person I can. I think that strength rubs off on others who might not be in the same boat.

We dressed up for road trips—and I am not talking suits, ties, and wingtip shoes. When we dressed in these crazy themed outfits for road trips—one trip, we had to paint our toenails if we elected to wear shorts and flip-flops—we all did it together. Nobody thought they were too "cool" to partake in the fun. Coaches, front office employees, everyone dressed up. The goofy outfits on road trips, the late batting practices on game days—even no batting practice on game days at times. It was about us. Joe really was good at making sure everyone shared in this little atmosphere of fun. It didn't feel like a workplace—more like a club that you loved being a member of.

Sometimes we just had to laugh at the whirlwind going on outside our little cocoon. We did a good job in 2016 of not letting those distractions creep into the clubhouse.

It was an amazing collection of people in the Cubs organization—not just the players—who made the 2016 season run smoothly. They allowed players to worry about nothing but baseball. It's a cool thing to know every person in the organization has your back.

The simple things make all the difference. Say if a player's "Aunt Sandy" was in town for a game, she requested an autographed ball from Anthony Rizzo. I simply went up to one of the clubhouse personnel and said, "Hey, can you give me a ball by Rizz?" Sure enough, boom, the ball was in your locker later that day and "Aunt Sandy" was thrilled. Sometimes it was even more basic. I was always pleased that the clubhouse guys made sure to have Starbucks iced coffee waiting for a few of us "old guys" every day.

Our protective cocoon worked so well almost nothing could rattle us, even Bill Murray. One night during the playoffs the actor/comedian suddenly rolled through the locker room. And then Vince Vaughn appeared, too. We had lots of big-time celebrities in the locker room. The thing was, Joe allowed folks like them to visit during the regular season. So it wasn't anything new. We took selfies with Bill Murray, and he told jokes. Vince Vaughn quoted his character from *Wedding Crashers*. You know, Rule 178: Never give up. Singer Chris Stapleton came in during the year, and country group Little Big Town visited.

All sorts of cool people came through the locker room. You might be thinking, Aren't these celebrities a big distraction? No. It was quite the opposite. They helped us forget about the far bigger distraction outside the clubhouse: the hopes and dreams of a few million Cubs fans.

• • • • • • • • • • • • • • •

DAVID'S iPHONE JOURNAL
2/23/16

Pretty cool day today. Last day before full squad, was light day for me. We did a warm-up with

Bussy, a fun throwing drill in our catchers early
work, catchers chat session, caught [Jake] Arrieta,
and took BP. Had a great lunch with my host family
from my first year (98) in Yakima Washington,
Sharron and Homer Applegate. We talked a lot
about that season and were trying to think of
everyone's name. I reminded her about making me
cinnamon toast after games because everything
was closed. They were a great host family and
helped me get my career started. Finished the
night with a "show" dinner with Demp, Wally, Lack,
Lester, and all the wives. Was a great night of food,
drinks, and stories! I really love those guys, they
have taught me so much! Really excited for full
squad tomorrow, can't wait to hear Joe's speech.

· · · · · · · · · · · · · · · · ·

Joe Maddon paid a great compliment to me after the season.
"I want to know who mentored David Ross," he said, "because
whoever taught David Ross to be what he was in our locker room
deserves a gold medal." Well, here's the answer, Joe: I am blessed
not just to have a single mentor or two. It was a culmination of positive influences in my life that turned me into the guy you saw in the
Cubs clubhouse. It started early in my career and centered on the
people I looked up to the most. My dad is a positive, don't-focus-
on-the-negative type of guy. I never once remember him raising his
voice at my mother. The older you get, you see flaws in people that
weren't apparent to you as a child. The truth is, I can't name for you
a flaw in my father. Another big childhood influence was my high

school baseball coach, Jeff Hogan, and I had some wonderful college coaches, too.

But the people who stand out for me as having the biggest positive impact on my outlook as a player are a group of guys I encountered during my fifteen-year career in the big leagues. Guys like Dave Roberts, Shawn Green, and Robin Ventura when I was with the Los Angeles Dodgers from 2002 to 2004. They taught me how to keep things loose, about having fun. Robin Ventura deserves a special mention. He never took himself too seriously. And here was a guy who was a two-time All-Star who played sixteen seasons in the big leagues.

Another highlight was my time in Atlanta from 2009 to 2012. After spending a few years on losing teams, where the morale could be low—and in turn, make players selfish—Atlanta was a big step for me in my development as a player, person, and teammate. Atlanta showed me what a good clubhouse culture was like.

I have to salute catcher Brian McCann. I get all emotional about that dude—he's just a quality human being to the core. Brian never says a bad word about anybody, even in private. After one early road game in Philadelphia he invited me to come hang out. I knocked on Brian's hotel door and he said, "Hey, come on in. I'm going to order room service." The postgame spread was sometimes terrible, so from then on we fell into a habit of ordering room service and talking baseball. Pitcher Eric O'Flaherty and first baseman Eric Hinske would show up, too, and we'd all sit around and talk about the game—and about life. Those little get-togethers made such a difference, especially on long road trips away from your family.

Pitcher Tim Hudson, my college teammate at Auburn, was in Atlanta, too. He's a great, great guy and friend. And I can't overlook manager Bobby Cox, a tremendous influence on me. Bobby knew how to get the most out of everyone. Atlanta was the first team I played for where the front office didn't tell its players how to act. Other organizations sometimes tell players *this is who you should be* and *this is how you should do it.* Atlanta was different. We didn't have a stretch time before games—it was the only organization I was in that didn't have a scheduled stretch time. It was the greatest thing ever. Bobby was like, "You're a professional and a grown man and you should know how to get yourself ready to play. I'm not going to tell you how to get ready." If I needed to stretch before a game, I went out and stretched. If you needed to take batting practice, you took batting practice.

Bobby expected you to look and act like a professional. We had a uniform we had to wear on and off the field. Bobby wanted you in slacks. That was about the only thing players hated about Bobby. We had to be dressed in slacks on the road with a collared shirt— the total opposite of Joe Maddon's philosophy! But the thing was, nobody in Atlanta complained about the dress code because Bobby allowed us to come and go as we wanted. There wasn't a curfew. He expected us as grown men to stay out of trouble, do things right, play hard.

When I returned to Boston in 2013, I saw what a winning organization looked like and what winning players believed in, what they did with their nights and downtime on the road. Some nights one of the guys might take out a guitar and we'd all hang out and have a beer together in the room—usually the suite of the player who made the most money! We'd have a few beers, play video games, talk. Dustin Pedroia, Mike Napoli, Jonny Gomes. Those guys invited me to their room to talk baseball. We talked strategy and how our team could get better. It also was an opportunity to get stuff off your chest, maybe even talk about your manager and a move he made in the game that night. These guys taught me how important open communication was in creating a good atmosphere and a winning ball club.

. . . .

DAVID'S iPHONE JOURNAL
2/26/16

Busy last few days, lots of dinners, golf, and hanging with the boys. Got Dex [Dexter Fowler] back yesterday, everyone was excited. Lost [Chris] Coghlin, I think he will get a great opportunity in Oakland. I'm getting a lot of attention about retiring and what great things my teammates are saying about me. Don't know why these guys love me so much but it sure feels nice. We are into live BP and the pitchers I caught look great. Feel ok in the box, BP is much more consistent. There are a bunch of great young kids in camp. The catching group has a bunch of great catchers.

. . . .

My journey in professional baseball began with the Los Angeles Dodgers. I was drafted in the seventh round out of Florida in the 1998 Major League Draft and made my major-league debut in 2002 at the age of twenty-five. Only three of the fifty players the Dodgers drafted in 1998 played for the big-league team four years later: first-rounder Bubba Crosby, fifth-rounder Scott Proctor, a product of Florida State in my hometown of Tallahassee, and me. I played in my first MLB game on June 29, 2002, pinch-hitting for Shawn Green and striking out in the ninth inning of a 7–0 loss to the Angels. Two months later, I doubled for my first major-league hit on September 2, 2002, at Arizona, off Eddie Oropesa. Later in the same game, I hit my first home run in the major leagues, off first baseman Mark Grace, who pitched the ninth inning in that game. We were beating the Diamondbacks 18–0 and Grace, a thirty-eight-year-old left-hander, volunteered to pitch the ninth inning. Grace retired Jeff Reboulet and Wilkin Ruan on fly-ball outs before I smacked a 396-foot home run to left field.

It's fun to reminisce about that at-bat. An ESPN story by Jesse Rogers in June 2016 recounted the historical moment with me and Mark, who still gives me grief to this day:

GRACE: I remember I got Jeff Reboulet out on a fly ball. I got Wilkin Ruan on a fly ball, then David Ross comes up. I never heard of the freaking guy. I figured he stinks.

ROSS: He threw a batting practice fastball, and Reboulet took it and he ended up getting him out. Then he did the same thing to the hitter in front of me. So I'm thinking to myself, if he lobs that in to me I'm swinging.

GRACE: Sure enough I threw him a 68 mph fastball down the middle and he tattooed it a long, long way.

ROSS: So he lobbed it in there and I hit it, man. I really hit it. I still have the bat. It's a Pro-Stock M110. You know, all these guys have their names on their bats and I have a Pro

Stock from the minors. So I'm sprinting around the bases and I hit first base and I hear him start screaming at me.

GRACE: I cursed at him all around the bases, then I realized after it was over that this poor son-of-gun waited his whole life to hit a home run in the big leagues, and of course he hits it off me in an 18–0 game.

ROSS: He's cursing, "C'mon man you're stealing my thunder." I'm keeping my head down like, oh my gosh, this guy is going to kill me. I was so nervous.

GRACE: I got a bad scouting report. I was told he was a good fastball hitter, so I threw a bad fastball and he still hit it a mile.

ROSS: It was over pretty quick, but the next day I got a request for a radio interview with him. I remember I was laughing the whole time and I let him talk. He was letting me have it. I probably didn't say five words.

GRACE: If I'm David Ross, I don't know if I wanted it any other way. How many guys can say their first big league home run was off a guy who threw one inning and was a position player for 16 years?

◇

In 2003, I became the Dodgers' backup catcher behind Paul Lo Duca when Todd Hundley underwent back surgery. I spent the final five months of 2003 on the big-league team, and 19 of my first 34 major league hits went for extra bases, including 11 home runs. According to *Dodger Insider*, I am the last Dodgers catcher with at least 100 plate appearances to slug above .500, so that's pretty cool. In 2004, I moved into the starter's role for the first time when Lo Duca was traded to the Florida Marlins on July 30.

I struggled at the plate that year, but one highlight of that season was my first walk-off home run. I hit a two-run home run in the bottom of the tenth inning off Steve Reed in a 4–2 win over the Colorado Rockies at Dodger Stadium in a game that clinched a tie for the National League West title. In the National League Division Series against St. Louis, I went 0-for-3 with a walk in a backup role behind veteran Brent Mayne. On March 30, 2005, during spring training after nearly seven years in the Dodgers organization, I was sold to the Pittsburgh Pirates.

Just when I thought I'd caught a break in getting promoted to the starting role, I had to pack my bags. Professional sports can be like that. As I headed off to Pittsburgh, I had no clue I was embarking on the start of a zigzag journey that would feature stops in Pittsburgh, San Diego, Cincinnati, Boston, Atlanta, Boston again, and, finally, Chicago.

CHAPTER 5

PUNCH IN THE GUT

8:15 P.M.

Cubs Lead, 1–0

Don't underestimate Kyle Hendricks.

Nicknamed "the Professor" by the media—we called him "Karl," though I was never quite sure how bullpen catcher Chad Noble came up with that name—Hendricks established himself as one of baseball's best control pitchers in 2016. The Ivy Leaguer could boast about his economics degree from Dartmouth College and a major league–best 2.13 ERA during the regular season. The right-handed starter entered Game 7 tied with Lew Burdett (1957) and Bob Gibson (1967) for the longest scoreless-inning streak in the postseason. Though he struggled to command his fastball in the early innings of Game Three, he threw four and a third scoreless innings in our 1–0 defeat.

Hendricks might not light up the radar gun, but he can throw a changeup, cutter, and curveball below the zone for strikes in fastball counts. Nearly 70 percent of his first pitches went for strikes in 2016, according to MLB metrics. Kyle might have flown under the radar in his second full season in the major leagues—he started the 2016 season as our number-five starter—but we knew he had the stuff and talent to be successful. His incredible 2016 season was probably my favorite story of the Cubs' season (not including my own, of course!).

After Dexter Fowler hit a solo home run to give us a 1–0 lead in the top of the first, Kyle set the Indians down in order in the bottom of the inning. Leadoff hitter Carlos Santana lined out to Jason Heyward in right field on Hendricks's first pitch. Hendricks struck out Jason Kipnis on a low changeup for the second out. Francisco Lindor reached first base on an error when second baseman Javier Baez slipped as he tried to throw from his knees after he fielded Lindor's ground ball. Hendricks avoided any potential trouble when he got a broken-bat ground-out to shortstop from Mike Napoli for the third out. It was just the start we were looking for.

◇

The cynic might say, well, it's easy to be a great teammate—*when you're winning.* I'd question that assumption. Is it easy to make sure everybody's happy and pulling on the same end of the rope? Is it easy to step back from your own problems and do the work of a good teammate?

Every player on our Cubs team had a job to do. I had a job to do, both in the clubhouse and on the field. If Joe Maddon called on me, I had to be ready. But I also learned that I needed to be able to recognize when spending some time with this guy or that guy could help. I wanted to be invested in every one of my teammates. For instance, there might be a day when I didn't like a player's body language. What's going on? He doesn't seem like he's into it today. On those occasions, I had to be direct and ask: Why are you not playing hard? What's going on? If a player is in a bad mood for three days, that affects our team and that affects me. If a player wasn't ready to play, it hurt our chance of winning. And I want to win.

If the end goal is winning, we should all be concerned about everybody.

Over my fifteen years in the big leagues, I developed a sixth sense for knowing when and how to approach my teammates. It stemmed from my own successes and failures as a player over many years. I was a starter at times, but mainly what we called "a role player." And there were stretches I was as bad as anyone could possibly be. But I also knew what success looked like. I was never a superstar, but I enjoyed success and thought, for a brief spell with the Cincinnati Reds, I had what it took to be a day-to-day starter for the long haul. That's not what panned out, of course. But those highs and lows—from watching and learning from the best and worst things that happened to me during my career—helped me develop my ability to connect with my teammates.

Sometimes you need a punch in the gut to help you gain perspective.

◇

Midway through my career, I reached a crossroad that changed my course in the major leagues as a player, a teammate, and as a person. In 2008, seven years into my big-league career, I was cut for the first time in the majors. The Cincinnati Reds released me on August 19. Manager Dusty Baker and I didn't see eye to eye, and I thought I deserved more playing time. Being released was a startling experience that, quite frankly, had me worried. I thought my career might be over.

I believed I had finally established myself as a starting catcher in the major leagues after I hit 38 home runs in my first two seasons (2006–07) in Cincinnati. I had landed in Cincinnati after abbreviated stops with the Pittsburgh Pirates and the San Diego Padres in 2005. The Dodgers sold me to Pittsburgh, where I played in thirty-five games in a reserve role before I was traded to San Diego in late July. I played in seven games with the Padres, who, the following spring training, traded me to the Reds for minor-league pitcher Bobby Basham on March 21, 2006.

That off-season, the Reds changed their ownership and their general manager. The team was managed by Jerry Narron. Right-handed pitcher Bronson Arroyo was an off-season pickup who would become a great friend. We finished in third place in the NL Central division, three and a half games behind the division winner and eventual World Series champion St. Louis Cardinals. At age twenty-nine, I was a starter and set career highs across the board in games (90), at-bats (247), doubles (15), home runs (21), and RBI (52). The 2007 season, however, didn't go as well for us as a team. Jerry Narron was fired on July 1, 2007, and advance scout Pete Mackanin was named the interim manager. We finished fifth in the NL Central behind Chicago, Milwaukee, St. Louis, and Houston.

The season, however, was a benchmark in my own play. I played 112 games—a career high. I also set a career high in at-bats (311) and I tied my career high in hits (61) from my previous season. My batting average dipped from .255 in 2006 to .203 in 2007, but I also hit 17 home runs and had 39 RBI. Defensively, I threw out 25 of 61 base stealers for a 41 percent rate, well above the league average of 25 percent. And my salary had tripled from $500,000 to $1.6 million annually in 2007, with an increase to $2.52 million in

2008. (My 2008 salary represented the highest to that point of my fifteen-year career.) I had a lot to feel good about after my first two seasons in Cincy.

In 2008 Dusty Baker came on board as the Reds' new manager. Dusty was a bit of a legend. He played nineteen years in the major leagues himself and previously managed the San Francisco Giants and the Chicago Cubs.

Dusty may have been a proven commodity, but he and I didn't get along at first. And when I was slowed by back spasms that started in spring training, that led to a platoon setup at catcher with Paul Bako. I wasn't happy about it. It felt like an insult after my successful first year in Cincinnati. I felt like I had finally hit my stride—I was hitting home runs, catching every day, partying with the guys. I was, in my own mind, one of the big-time players in Cincinnati.

I let the ego thing get me. And then, all of a sudden, I wasn't playing as much as I thought I deserved. I went into a hitting slump. Still, I was pissed about the situation and I complained to Dusty.

Big mistake.

On August 19, 2008—at age thirty-one and after appearing in only fifty-two games that season—I was released. It really humbled me in a hurry. It happened in the snap of a finger. Just as I'd started to believe the hype and was sucked into it, I now worried my playing career might be done.

Three days later, to my relief, I signed a free agent contract with the Boston Red Sox and ended up finishing the season on a team that finished second in the American League East (the Reds, by contrast, finished second to last in the NL Central). Led by manager Terry Francona, the Sox beat the Angels in the American League Division Series before losing to Tampa Bay in the American

League Championship Series in seven games. The team boasted a great group of guys, including Dustin Pedroia, David Ortiz, Jason Varitek, and many others.

I only played in eight games that season for the Sox and had a measly one hit in eight at-bats, but I embraced the environment and the organization's culture of winning. I also immediately felt at home. I was the team's third-string catcher but I got to attend the advance meetings heading into the 2008 playoffs—not always the case for a "reserve" catcher. I wasn't afraid to speak up and offered my insights—with conviction and confidence—on our own pitchers' strengths and how we should attack hitters in the two series against the Angels and the Rays. It was wonderful to be someplace that sought and welcomed my opinion, but I knew I likely was just a short-term "rental" for the Red Sox.

After losing to Tampa Bay, I was in the Red Sox locker room packing to head home to Florida for the off-season when Theo Epstein, the team's general manager and executive vice president, walked up to me. He motioned me into Terry Francona's empty office. Theo told me he loved that I was part of the organization and he'd be in touch in the off-season. Even at that time, Theo told me I'd make a great coach or front office staffer when my playing career had ended. I was a free agent, and Theo was up front about the team's plan to re-sign starting catcher Jason Varitek. Jason was the team's All-Star captain who, at that point, had played all twelve of his major-league seasons with Boston. Theo said he'd keep me posted and I appreciated his honesty.

Then, just as I was about to head back to my locker, Theo made a comment that blindsided me. He said it was a comment I deserved to hear. Theo told me the word out of Cincinnati was that "David Ross is a bad teammate."

A bad teammate?

My eyes got wide and I just stood there for a moment in stunned silence. A bad teammate? That went against every fiber in my soul. Thoughts raced through my head—Who could have said that? And why would they say it? But I was too stunned to ask; too stunned, frankly, to say anything. I just listened. According to the grapevine, Theo said, in Cincinnati I had a difficult time accepting my role and instead acted more like a "me-guy" in the clubhouse. Theo stressed he had not seen that from me in Boston, but he wanted me to know about it.

The "bad teammate" comment cut deeply because I didn't see myself that way. Yes, I definitely had shown I was a little self-absorbed when I was in Cincinnati—it was the first time in my career I was an everyday catcher and I believed I had earned it. I was invested in myself and trying to do the best I could. Was that being a bad teammate? I was flummoxed. Theo said it was difficult for him to imagine I could be a bad teammate, but he felt I needed to know as I headed into free agency and contemplated my future. "Reputations die hard," he said. "And that's yours by some account."

Whether it was a fair label or not, I realized at that moment I didn't want that to be my reputation.

Looking back on it, walking into Cincinnati manager Dusty Baker's office when I was pissed off and wanting more playing time when the team had just suffered a loss probably didn't look good. But I was tired of being lied to and didn't know what my role was with the team. I was mad and frustrated. I acted out.

I learned a lot from that bad decision, and Theo's message helped me take it to heart. I was forever grateful to Theo for being so honest.

You have to put the team first, not yourself. I hadn't done that in my conversation with Dusty, and I hadn't done it in Cincinnati.

Big lesson learned.

I could have gotten defensive, or laughed off the criticism. Instead, that conversation with Theo in an empty office became a turning point for me: As I headed into the 2008 off-season, I needed to figure out how never to let those words be said about me again. Wherever I landed, I was committed to becoming the best team-mate I could possibly be.

· · · · · · · · · · · · · · · ·

DAVID'S iPHONE JOURNAL
2/29/16

Really miss my family

· · · · · · · · · · · · · · · ·

After I finished out the season in Boston, my agent, Ryan Gleichowski, and I talked about my options. Ryan and I were baseball teammates at the University of Florida, and Ryan's wife, Rose, and I attended the same high school, Florida High, in Tallahassee—further proof that it's a small world. (There's actually a photo floating around of Rose and me at Florida High's middle school prom.) Ryan and Marc R. Pollack formed Sports One Athlete Management in 1999, and I was Ryan's first professional client. I signed with Ryan when I was in Single-A in Vero Beach with the Los Angeles Dodgers in 1999, and we've been together ever since.

One of the early options we talked about for the 2009 sea-son was a one-year deal with the Houston Astros as a starter. The

Atlanta Braves were in the mix, too, making me a two-year, $3 million offer as the backup to All-Star catcher Brian McCann.

Like any professional baseball player, I always wanted to try to make the best decision from a business standpoint but also one that enabled me to continue to play my best, to contribute as much as I could. I never wanted to get too greedy, and I always wanted to be in the right situation. I certainly wanted to take care of myself and my family financially—but not to the point of ultimate risk. I always knew that this life was not going to last forever.

Ryan wanted me to pursue the one-year offer with Houston to prove that I could continue to be a starter. If I had a big year, like banging twenty home runs, then maybe I would get even a bigger payday the following year. The Braves offered a little more money and security, but I also understood the ramifications. I was pretty much signing up to be a backup catcher the rest of my career. But you know what? I was good with it. I knew my role and made the decision to embrace it. The grass is not always greener on the other side, right? I'd been a backup for most of my career. I had the chance to start in Cincinnati and look what happened. This was a new opportunity with the Braves, a chance to turn the page. And, most important, my role was defined for me.

Brian McCann was the starter, I was his backup. There was no gray area. It wasn't a competition between the two of us. I think one of the hardest things as a baseball player, at least for me, was not knowing my role. In Cincinnati Dusty didn't define it for me sufficiently. It wasn't a good feeling to walk into the Cincinnati clubhouse every day and look at the lineup wondering, Am I playing today? (Nowadays they send out the lineup via text message.)

All professional athletes are amazing competitors. Many have been blessed with tremendous physical abilities, tremendous insights, and tremendous mental toughness. Everyone is wired differently, however, and I think one characteristic that separates the ones who stay for a long period of time from the ones who don't stick around is what happens from the shoulders up. I think my ability to understand and embrace my role—and to be the best at that role—is one of the single most important factors for my long-term success on and off the field.

On December 5, 2008, I signed with the Atlanta Braves.

As much as it was a pivotal time in my career, my transition to the Braves was seamless. Brian McCann and I hit it off immediately. He's become one of my closest friends. Brian and I knew of each other prior to my signing with the Braves, though. It's a funny story, but we almost got into an altercation during a game with the Braves when I was with the Reds. Brian said something to one of our hitters about trying to bunt for a hit when his pitcher had a no-hitter going, so I started screaming at him from the top step of our dugout. If I would have been in his shoes, I may have done the same thing. But this was my teammate and I stick up for my guy no matter what.

Brian had made the All-Star team three consecutive seasons when I joined the Braves. Backing up a player of Brian's caliber was the best thing for me at that point in my career. Seeing how he worked with pitchers and thought so differently, being a great hitter, took my game to a whole new level.

Brian and I got along so well because we had similar attitudes toward the game. It felt like we became best friends instantly. And I liked the routine in Atlanta. I knew the days I was scheduled to play to give Brian a break. I got the opportunity to learn the pitching staff. I was really fond and appreciative of the communication within the organization. And Atlanta was close to my hometown of Tallahassee, so it was an easy trip for family and friends. Not to mention I had the chance to play for the legendary Bobby Cox, who was nearing the end of his Hall of Fame coaching career.

. . . .

DAVID'S iPHONE JOURNAL
3/3/16

Well, it's been a crazy few days. Camp is in full swing and we started games today. They had a crazy retirement prank/gift thing for me this morning. It was pretty funny, gave me a grocery store scooter and a golf cart thing that carries my bag!! I told Kyle I'd name it Schwarber and he said, "I am honored." I love that kid. These past few days I have been busy. We had a team golf outing, dinner and golf with Lack and Millar three days in a row. Got to meet and golf with Michael Waltrip. He is hilarious. Getting things lined up for the family to get out here. They are changing so fast, I can't wait to see them. Got a few nights out with my wife planned. I can't wait to talk to her. She is having a hard time running the family solo. I can't imagine that for a long period of time. I am excited/nervous about the first game tomorrow. Will be fun to see how much more (work) I need.

. . . .

Atlanta was such a special place for me. We averaged 90 wins over my four seasons with the Braves. In July 2010, the Braves signed me to another two-year extension for $3.25 million. Fredi Gonzalez replaced Bobby Cox, who retired following the 2010 season, as the manager.

We had a special group of guys there. Brian McCann, Eric Hinske, Eric O'Flaherty, and I formed a unique bond. We all spent many nights in each other's hotel rooms, talking about the game, about strategies, about getting the most out of our pitchers, about life. I was nicknamed "Sensei" by my Braves teammates because, well, if they ever needed an answer or an opinion, they'd get it from me. (When McCann added my contact information to his cell phone, he labeled it "Sensei.") I was brutally honest, too, and probably said some things to my teammates that might have resulted in a right cross to the chin from guys who didn't know me. But I cared about everyone and tried to get the best out of them, Brian included.

Every half inning in my four years in Atlanta, I greeted Brian with a high-five from the top step of the dugout as he came off the field. Brian did the same for me, with one exception. He missed the start of one game and wasn't at the top of the step to greet me when I came in from the top of the first inning. Well, I lit into him. "I meet you at the top step before every game and you can't come out when I play?" I said. Brian felt terrible. "Dude, I'm sorry. It won't ever happen again." And it never did.

I never was a player who did well when I competed with a teammate. I always looked at it like the catching corps should be the tightest group on the team. And it was that way in Atlanta.

When I went into a backup role in Atlanta, it was easier for me to focus on what the group needed rather than think only of myself.

And the feeling wasn't limited to my role with the Braves. I never thought of myself as a bad person, or a bad teammate or a bad guy. But the switch flipped in Atlanta and I consciously wanted to be a better husband, a better friend, a better teammate, a better man. Being around guys like Brian made me a better man.

Not playing every day helped me, too. I could spend more time with my family, spend more time with the kids in the pool, and be a better dad and not worry about being tired later that night.

As I said, winning is about everyone pulling on the same end of the rope. In the Braves' 2012 play-in game (the winner advanced into the division series) against the St. Louis Cardinals, Fredi benched Brian in favor of me. Slowed by a shoulder injury, Brian batted just .230 with 20 home runs and 67 RBIs, numbers well below his All-Star average. Fredi said he made the move for defense, saying I had the better chance of keeping the Cardinals from attempting to steal. Brian and I talked about it. I know it hurt him but he wanted what was best for the team. Brian wanted to catch in that game, but he said it didn't take long for him to get over it—maybe ten minutes—because he knew I was behind the plate. I appreciated his support.

Kris Medlen was scheduled to start the game against the Cardinals, and I had been behind the plate for two of his best performances that year—a 12-strikeout effort against Colorado on September 3 and a career-high 13 strikeouts against Washington on September 14. I made an immediate impact in the game when I hit a two-run home run to center in the second inning on a 1-2 count from Cardinals starter Kyle Lohse. But the Cardinals quickly rallied and led 6–2 in the fifth inning. We eventually lost the game 6–3. The game also marked the end of the Hall of Fame career of Braves third baseman Chipper Jones, who had spent his entire nineteen years in Atlanta. While news of my departure two months later didn't garner the same headlines (imagine that!), I had established myself as one of the best backup catchers in Major League Baseball during my four years with the Braves.

More important, I had evolved into a valuable teammate.

◇

During the 2015 National League playoffs, Dusty Baker and I had the chance to talk. He told me he'd listened too much to people who influenced his decision to cut my playing time in Cincinnati. And I told him I'd realized I'd made mistakes and didn't handle the situation well. We talked things out and all is good between us today.

Looking back on it, 2008 was the best thing that could have ever happened to me. It was then that I learned what the word *teammate* really meant.

CHAPTER 6

BEST SEAT IN THE HOUSE

8:45 P.M.

Cubs Lead, 1–0

Facing Kyle Hendricks on the mound, Cleveland's Coco Crisp led off the bottom of the third with a double down the left-field line. Roberto Perez followed with a sacrifice bunt that advanced Crisp to third. On a 1-0 count, Carlos Santana stayed back on a curveball and laced a single to right field to easily score Crisp and tie the game.

The Indians appeared poised for a big inning when we muffed a potential inning-ending double-play ball. Jason Kipnis hit a ground ball to shortstop Addison Russell that caught the lip of the infield grass and dirt. But Addy fielded the ball cleanly and flipped it to Javier Baez at the bag. Javier tried to catch it barehanded with his right hand as he crossed the bag, but he dropped the ball. Santana was initially called out, but after an official's review of the play, all runners were ruled safe.

Emotions are running so high and you are locked into every pitch. My heart was already racing, and now things looked like they were going to get a little hairy. Hendricks fell behind 2-0 to Francisco Lindor. Our pitching coach, Chris Bosio, made a mound visit as relievers Mike Montgomery and Carl Edwards Jr. started to throw in the bullpen. After Hendricks threw ball three to Lindor, the young left-handed hitter swung away and fouled the next pitch back for strike one. He flied out to left field on the next pitch for the second out. That brought up Mike Napoli, who worked the count to 1-2 but lined out to Kris Bryant at third base to end the threat.

◇

I considered it the greatest of compliments when, following my retirement, some of my peers raised the notion that I might be a worthy candidate to manage a Major League Baseball team. I gained valuable experience from playing under some of the great managers, guys like Joe Maddon, Bobby Cox, Bruce Bochy, Terry Francona, and John Farrell, among others.

It's true that my behavior on the bench as a player could be a bit manager-like at times. When I was on the bench, I was always trying to figure out a way to beat the other team. I'd think about what coaches and players on other teams I'd like to have on my team if I were the manager. I always observed the opposing team to see how they handled themselves and played the game. That was always fun to me.

During Cubs games, I sat behind the dugout rail between assistant hitting coach Eric Hinske and first base coach Brandon Hyde. When we were on defense, I picked their brains and talked strategies. Eric always stood in the stairwell toward the back of the dugout and I sat next to him on a stool. Anytime a situation came up in the game, I asked Eric, "What would you do right here?" or "Why would you do this?" He asked me the same questions, and we went back and forth like that over the entire course of the season.

Apart from the squatting, playing catcher was the best seat in the house as far as I was concerned. I also wanted to be in that seat to show my teammates I was invested in them and cared about how they played that day. I wanted to do everything I could to help us win.

My teammates knew they had to be on their toes around me. Professional baseball is not a real rah-rah game, like European soccer or even the NFL or NBA. But I was loud. I always tried to yell positive encouragement from the dugout—you know, some "attaboys!"—and cheer for the guys. I also always tried to make sure my teammates were doing the right thing. I didn't want them messing up because I wanted to win. Physical errors are part of the game; everyone makes them, and I made my share during my fifteen years in the major leagues. But I wanted to make sure the guys didn't repeat mental errors. Like where a player was supposed to be on this play or this count. What's the situation? What are we trying to get done here? It was always "we." Selfishness doesn't work in baseball. There are times when players had to sacrifice themselves and give up an at-bat to advance a runner or to score a run. I think managers watched for the same things.

There was a time when major-league teams seemingly only hired a manager who had managed in the big leagues before. That is no longer the norm. For instance, from 2010 to 2013, fifteen new managers had no—or virtually no—previous big-league experience. My good friend and former Los Angeles Dodgers teammate Robin Ventura was among that group when he was hired by the

Chicago White Sox in 2012. Another good friend, Dave Roberts, led the Los Angeles Dodgers to the National League Championship Series in his first season in 2016 after he served as the bench coach in San Diego for six years. (We beat Dave and the Dodgers in six games in the NLCS.)

Mike Matheny of the St. Louis Cardinals probably has enjoyed the most success as a first-time manager. I've always believed catchers make good managers because they are involved in every pitch and just about every aspect of the game. It's the only position where you face the entire field, every play and decision is in front of you. A catcher who played thirteen years with four organizations, Mike coached Little League baseball after his playing career ended. The Cardinals hired him following the 2011 season and in 2015 he became the first manager in Major League Baseball history to lead his team to the playoffs in each of his first four seasons.

Joe Maddon's career path was much different, and his advice to me if I really wanted to be a big-league manager was to get into the game first as a scout or as a manager at the minor-league level. Joe was a catcher in the minors, but he never made it higher than Class A. He worked in the Angels organization for thirty-one years and wore a number of different hats. He was a minor-league manager, a scout, a roving minor-league hitting instructor, and an assistant coach on the major-league team. His first chance to manage on the big-league level was with the Tampa Bay Rays from 2006 through 2014, winning the 2008 American League pennant, before he opted out of his contract and signed with the Cubs. Joe said scouting was probably the most important part of his background. That's because he knows what a player looks like at a young age and he knows how to be patient.

Managing a Major League Baseball team is no walk in the park. You have to deal with big personalities, find the right match-ups, and maximize players' talents.

I think Joe nailed it too on how we needed to handle our emotions after games. He wanted players to respect their teammates in wins and losses. We may have won a game but maybe one particular player had a bad day at the plate or made an error on the field, and didn't feel good about himself. Maddon's approach was give that guy thirty minutes to gather his thoughts. Then, by the time you got to the car or on the plane, it was "Let it go, let it go. We have tomorrow." That might be easier said than done, but I thought players grew into that mindset. It worked for me, and I encouraged it. And as a veteran, to help set that example, I always reminded the guys, "Did you do your best? Let's learn from our mistakes and move on."

Joe often used the word *authentic* when he described me and the 2016 Cubs team. Joe believed that 95 percent or more of players and employees on our team were authentic. He also knew that I didn't bullshit people. I was straight up with everyone. I was blunt and, at times, a sledgehammer. Joe told me that quality would benefit me if I were to become a manager. But he also always tried to impart on me that "honesty without compassion can equal cruelty at times." He believed that if I became a manager I would need to lighten the message a bit on occasion. As a player, I could be as blunt as I wanted to be and players accepted it. But being a manager was different. He was blunt, but he wasn't blunt in a manner that felt oppressive. If that happened, he felt he could start losing a player or have him so concerned about what Joe was thinking or saying to him that he couldn't refocus on his game.

Of course, I didn't always agree with Joe's decisions as a manager, especially when he lifted me for a pinch hitter in games that I started. When I only got four at-bats a week or so as a backup, I wanted every single one! (Unless it was some nasty closer throwing gas; then someone else could have it.)

In Game Five of the World Series at Wrigley Field, I was frustrated about being lifted for a pinch hitter (Miguel Montero) in the bottom of the sixth inning. Jon Lester started for us on the mound and went six innings, and Joe had decided to go to the bullpen for the seventh (Carl Edwards Jr. got one out in the seventh, and Aroldis Chapman threw the final two and two-thirds innings in the 3–2 victory that sent the Series back to Cleveland). I had a couple of good at-bats and knocked in our third run with a sacrifice fly in the three-run fourth inning to erase a 1–0 deficit. Joe knew I wasn't happy but I wasn't going to be negative about it either. Still, later that night on the charter flight to Cleveland, Joe fired me a text that read, "Hey brother . . . my screw up . . . didn't process everything. . . . I am sorry." It was a small gesture, but it meant a lot to me.

Probably the toughest conversation I ever had with Joe during my two seasons with the Cubs happened in 2015. It only was the eleventh game of the season—and my eleventh game with the Cubs—and we played an afternoon game at Wrigley against the San Diego Padres. Jon Lester had started the game and was lifted with one out in the top of the sixth. I was scheduled to lead off the bottom of the sixth—we trailed 3–2 at the time—and Joe lifted me for a pinch hitter who was a young prospect. I had walked my previous two times at the plate and thought I saw the ball pretty well. The pinch hitter struck out and we eventually lost the game 5–2. I was ticked about being lifted and really didn't understand the move. It wasn't anything against the pinch hitter but I didn't think hitting him gave us the best chance to win. I wouldn't have minded if it had been Miggy Montero or somebody else, but the prospect had been struggling, batting .077 in eleven games.

Joe sensed I was upset so he called me into his office after the game. He said, "Let's talk, you good?" I said, "Yeah, I'm good." Of course, Joe knew I wasn't. He wanted to talk and he wanted the conversation to be open and candid, man to man. That was nice to hear, especially since some of my manager talks in the past had not gone well for me. I told Joe I didn't understand his move to have the young prospect hit for me. I said, "I'm watching the same game you are and he's not having good at-bats. He's been lost at the plate his last few at-bats and I didn't think he gave us a better chance to win." Joe answered and said he wanted to get him some at-bats. Before Joe could get out another word, I stopped him. "Whoa. Okay, I'm talking to the wrong guy then," I said. "If we're here to get guys at-bats, I'm in the wrong place. I signed with the wrong team, and I need to go talk to Theo [Epstein] and get out of here."

I told Joe that my response wasn't anything against him. But I wanted him to know if the plan in place was to get guys at-bats, then I was in the wrong place. I wasn't here for that; I came to win. I was grateful Joe allowed me to speak openly. I was a little nervous when I left his office. But I didn't need to be. Joe's plan all along had probably been to simply let me get it off of my chest and say my piece. That's why he's so great; he doesn't let things stew.

When I came up early in my career, it always seemed there was a separation between the coaches and the front office and the players. The best organizations I played for, like the Cubs, were places where everybody worked together and depended on one another. In those organizations, the coaches and front offices would ask for honest feedback from the players. There was a give-and-take, and it felt like everyone was on the same page, all working toward the common goal of winning. When everyone communicates, everyone is on the same page and pulling together. There were some organizations that were secretive, but Chicago wasn't one of them.

· · · · · · · · · · · · · · · ·

DAVID'S iPHONE JOURNAL
3/16/16

Busy week, family in town. Had Cole and my Dad at the field with me the last few days. Cole is getting much better. I am much happier with them here, feel complete. Think I like hanging with Hyla the most. Miss our time to catch up. She truly is my best friend. Got to hang with Brett Eldredge and his brother Brice for a few days. They came over to Lester's and sang while we played guitar. Was one of the best nights yet. Baseball is going well. Guys are starting to play together more now that they are making cuts. We have a lot of talent at all levels. Very impressive. Think guys are starting to get excited about the season. I know I am. Pitchers are starting to get stretched out and hit. I have been playing much better this week. Arm feeling much better and feel good at the plate. Got a birthday coming up Saturday. Will be 39! Hadn't thought about it until we went to dinner for Caitlyn Motte's birthday last night.

· · · · · · · · · · · · · · · ·

I can't talk about managers without saying a few more words about Bobby Cox, the Hall of Fame coach who happens to be one of the nicest human beings I have ever met. Bobby was so positive and really cared about the players and everyone within the Atlanta Braves organization. Now, don't get me wrong, he was really competitive, too. There's a reason why he is ranked fourth all-time on baseball's managerial win list with 2,504, behind Connie Mack (3,731), John McGraw (2,763), and Tony La Russa (2,728). I can still remember a game with the Braves when we were getting blown out—I think it was against Philadelphia, with Roy Halladay on the mound. We were down big early and it only got worse. It was one of those games where you try to play it out and "Hey, let's go get 'em tomorrow." After the last out of the game was made, Bobby was down at the end of the dugout with the lineup card in his hand. As he walked down the steps into the locker room, he dropped an F-bomb and threw his lineup card to the ground. I was like, "What the hell?" I had been checked out of the game mentally by the third inning. But Bobby's reaction showed me how much confidence he had in the team and that he managed until the last out, no matter what the scoreboard read. No matter what the scoreboard said, Bobby always looked and thought that somehow, someway we would find a way to come back and win that game.

In Chicago, we had hitters' meetings and a pitchers' meeting separately where we went over individual scouting reports. In Atlanta, meetings before games were held in the locker room and all the players attended. Coaches would go over how we intended to pitch to this guy or how we intended to play that guy. Both the pitching coach and the hitting coach would usually talk. Bobby always started each meeting with a short message, where he'd say something like, "Hey, guys, you are playing really good, keep it up," or "Hey, I know we're going through a rough stretch but I see you guys are playing hard and I really appreciate it. Keep doing what you're doing and we'll come out of this." It was a quick message, but it was always a confidence builder. If we were struggling at that time, we knew from his message that he wasn't down on us and believed in us.

Bobby wasn't ever-present. He would hole up in his office, out of your way, or hunker in the tunnel smoking a cigar right before the game. But when he talked, it was purposeful—and he always had something positive to say. That was his manner, his personality. Bobby might have seen me in the food room and said, "Hey, Rossy, way to go." As a player, you might think, What did I do? I didn't get a hit last night. But I appreciated that the Skipper was fired up for me. It was a simple but effective way in which he changed your mindset.

I remembered one game where I went 0-for-4 with three punch-outs and didn't even sniff the pitcher. Bobby stood on that dugout perch during games and he'd pat players on the shoulder or say something quick. I was down about my at-bat as I walked by Bobby, who said, "Man, Rossy, that guy is nasty today." Bobby had a way to send a positive message even under negative circumstances, and that really stood out to me. Once, when we were in the middle of an eleven-game losing streak, I remember Bobby saying, "Guys, I know we are going through a rough stretch but we have twenty-three, twenty-four guys playing hard and we need all twenty-five. And if we can't have all twenty-five, there's plenty of guys in the minor leagues that will want to come up here."

It was Bobby's polite way of telling us to get it together. Even when you're losing, that doesn't mean you stop playing hard. We should never lose focus of what we are doing. Bobby always told us that when we hit that clubhouse door, whatever happened that morning or that afternoon or the night before was all history. He wanted players to walk into that clubhouse with a smile—and to be ready to go to work.

. . . .

DAVID'S iPHONE JOURNAL
3/23/16

WOW!!! What a busy time with my family! We did so much. Top golf, movie, hiking, lots of pool time, great team parties, and a few nights out with mamma! This has been the best spring of my life. Doing more than ever before and feels great. Joe really looks out for his players. Probably why his teams always play well late in the year. Think the kids had a great trip, feel bad for Hyla going home with two kids and a newborn. All that being said, it feels like everyone is starting to dial it up a bit. Camp's getting smaller and drills are running smooth. Our lineup looks really nice. Jeff Passan wrote a nice "Grandpa Rossy" article. Going to Lakers game tonight with Dex!

. . . .

Bobby Cox never considered me a backup during my two seasons with him even though I was signed to back up Brian McCann. Bobby looked at me as an everyday guy. He liked the way I caught, managed pitchers, and managed the game. I rediscovered my power stroke in Atlanta. Bobby hadn't heard about the rumor that had started in Cincinnati about me being a bad teammate. But it was under Bobby and in Atlanta that I really hit the turning point in my career. You know, you have to ask yourself, Do I want to go home or do I want to embrace what is happening to me? I checked my ego at the door every day and asked myself what I could do to help this team win. Under Bobby and the Braves, I understood I had value. But, even more important, I also watched how Bobby managed the game and managed people. He was a huge influence for me, just watching how he communicated with everyone. Bobby knew everyone's name. That really made an impression on me and it's where I started to take the same approach of making sure I introduced myself and said hello to everyone within the organization.

Bobby knew everyone, down to the ushers and the guys who were cleaning the seats. From the top of the organization all the way down to the bottom, Bobby treated everyone equally. And he always had a nice word to say to everyone. During games, some managers always seemed to have their minds made up. But I felt like Bobby and Joe did a great job of watching the game. They let the game dictate what they wanted to do. If you watch the game intently, a lot of times it makes the decision for you.

CHAPTER 7

MIKE NAPOLI AT THE PLATE

8:58 P.M.

Game Tied, 1–1

It wasn't a surprise that first baseman Mike Napoli was a big part of Cleveland's success in 2016, on and off the field.

Earlier in the game, in the bottom of the first inning, right-hander Kyle Hendricks worked around an error and got Napoli on a broken-bat ground ball to shortstop Addison Russell for the third out. And in the bottom of the third, Napoli lined out to third baseman Kris Bryant to end the Indians' scoring threat.

Napoli is a winner, and a great friend. He's a fun guy to be around. Nap didn't have a great Series, but he was one of the Indians' best power hitters most of the year and finished the season with career highs in home runs (34) and RBIs (101).

I know what Nap brought to the table when we (along with Cubs teammates Jon Lester and John Lackey) won the World Series with the Boston Red Sox in 2013. Napoli was a key addition to the team. He quickly became a leader and helped transform the Red

Sox clubhouse. He never gave away an at-bat. He could always find a way to work the count to 3–2 and have a quality at-bat.

◇

I became a free agent in October 2012 after my fourth and final year in Atlanta.

The Red Sox showed immediate interest. I had played in the organization briefly in 2008 following my release from the Reds. Ben Cherington, executive vice president and general manager of the Red Sox, reached out to my agent, Ryan Gleichowski, and said I was the perfect fit in what he wanted to build in Boston in 2013. Cherington was aggressive in his approach, too. They put the full court press on me.

It had been a difficult few years for the Red Sox organization but I wasn't worried about what happened in the past. John Farrell was hired as the team's new manager—he replaced Bobby Valentine—on October 21, 2012, and I understood Cherington was really determined to rebuild the team for 2013. Plus I knew John from my time in Boston in 2008, when he was the pitching coach, and enjoyed him.

I always instructed Chow (my agent, Ryan Gleichowski) never to jump the gun in negotiations. We would both know when the situation was right. We never really wanted to put a specific time frame on negotiations. The situation had to be right and we had to feel good about it: the contract, the commitment, and even geographically, for my family. When it was right, we knew it.

And Boston felt right.

Still, since it was so early in the free agent market that off-season, I was anxious to see what kind of commitment Boston wanted to make to me. Cherington said he was focused on talent, but he wanted talent that included "character." He wanted guys who cared about each other as much as they cared about winning.

I still vividly remember when the Boston Red Sox made me an offer to return to the team. I was driving down the street in my hometown of Tallahassee. I was on Bannerman Road, not too far from my home, when Ben called my cell phone. It was a three-way call between myself, Chow, and Ben. When Ben started to talk numbers, I immediately pulled into a Chevron gas station. I was like, "Are you kidding me?"

I sat in my car near the car wash at the gas station because I wanted to make sure I never lost this call because it was one of those amazing moments. I realized that being a solid person had actually suddenly become really valuable to me, and it was more money than I had ever been offered at one time. It was an over-whelming moment. I didn't want to lose the call because I wasn't sure I had heard Ben right. I had.

On November 12, 2012, I signed a two-year, $6.2 million deal. It was the most lucrative contract of my career—and to show how far I had come, it was a huge improvement over my rookie year salary of $310,000 with the Los Angeles Dodgers in 2004. It was reported by the media that my return was "more than a backup but not a starter" behind Jarrod Saltalamacchia. The Red Sox also had a young, talented catcher in Ryan Lavarnway.

But it was about more than salary and the depth chart.

For the first time, I was a real priority. There were other teams involved but the Red Sox brass made it clear: "Hey, we really, really want you. You're number one on our list." The Red Sox said they had a Plan A and a Plan B, and Plan A started with me. That meant so much to me. I was their number-one target as a backup. That's weird, right? The Tampa Bay Rays were in the mix, too, and my wife, Hyla, wanted to go to Tampa so bad. Her sister had recently moved to Tampa from Tallahassee. The two cities are 275 miles apart, and playing close to home would have been nice. It's only a four-hour drive but the Rays were about one million dollars short in salary, and a million dollars is a million dollars (especially when you know your first career has an early expiration date).

And the Red Sox are the Red Sox.

Ben signed seven key free agents in November and December 2012: myself, former Oakland Athletics outfielder Jonny Gomes, former Rangers and Angels catcher/first baseman Mike Napoli, former Phillies and Dodgers outfielder Shane Victorino, former Baltimore Orioles and Rangers relief pitcher Koji Uehara, former Arizona Diamondbacks and Athletics shortstop Stephen Drew, and former Texas starter Ryan Dempster, who had been traded by the Cubs to the Rangers in July 2012 at the trade deadline. And with the return of core players such as David Ortiz, Jacoby Ellsbury, Jon Lester, and John Lackey, all the pieces were in place for a helluva season.

. . . .

DAVID'S iPHONE JOURNAL
3/4/16

Made a great play today in first game. Coolest thing was the looks on my coaches' faces and a high-five from everyone in the dugout. Felt like I high-fived 60 people. My son said to me today after his baseball practice, "Dad, in Arizona, can we have boy time and throw and catch the ball?"

. . . .

It was a remarkable season in so many ways.

After Boston finished last in the American League East in 2012, we became the eleventh team in major-league history to go from worst in the division to first the next season when we clinched the AL East division title in September. At 97-65, we had the best record in the American League and tied the St. Louis Cardinals for the best record in baseball.

We went on to beat the Cardinals four games to two to capture the organization's eighth World Series. We were the first team since the 1991 Minnesota Twins to win the Series after finishing in last place. And, for the first time, Boston defeated the same franchise twice to win the Series.

I had the game-winning hit in Game Five and caught the final pitch in Game Six that saw us clinch the title at Fenway Park for the first time in ninety-five years. Lifting reliever Koji Uehara into the air in celebration after he struck out Matt Carpenter for that final out is an image and feeling I will always remember. And I still have that baseball. I tucked it in my back pocket as I ran to the mound. Nobody from the Red Sox ever asked me for it, and I have it in a glass case on the mantel in my Tallahassee home. (Hope they don't ask for it after they read this!)

We had such a tight group of players. In spring training earlier that season, Napoli and Gomes started to grow out their beards. It caught on with many of the players, and our beards were a rallying point for players and fans. We tugged on each other's beards in celebration and many fans wore real or fake beards to games in our honor. And I'll never forget how much—from day one of spring training—our group talked about winning the World Series.

I'd never been around a team that talked about winning the World Series as much as we did that year. From the first day of spring training, guys talked about winning the World Series. We had shirts made at the All-Star break with a duck boat on the back. It was just another day closer to the World Series victory parade using those tourist boats in Boston. Literally, we talked like that the entire season.

That mentality started with second baseman Dustin Pedroia. This guy makes everybody better! In spring training in 2013, team president Larry Lucchino asked Dustin in the hallway, "How do you think we are going to do this year?" And in his matter-of-fact way, Peddy (pronounced "PD") said, "We're going to win the World Series!" Larry said he would buy him a car if we did. Dustin is now the proud owner of a sick Ford Raptor!

It was a tough year, too.

I missed sixty-five games after I suffered two concussions within a month's span. For the second time, I thought my career might be over. It was a lonely place, being sent back home in Talla-hassee for two months and not knowing if the game I loved might be taken away. It was a dark time for me. But thanks to the help and support of a lot of people, my family, good doctors, and the Red Sox organization, I returned in August and contributed to our Series title.

The other reason it was a tough time came from the outside world. On April 15—Patriots Day—two pressure cooker bombs exploded twelve seconds apart at 2:49 p.m. in the middle of the crowd that had gathered at the finish line of the Boston Marathon. The terror attack killed three spectators and injured 264 others. Two police offers also died during the pursuit of the suspects.

We beat Tampa Bay at Fenway Park earlier that afternoon to sweep the Rays and close out a six-game home stand, and we headed to Cleveland later that day without really knowing what had happened. We'd heard that something bad had happened, but nobody knew the specifics at that time. We were on the team buses, headed to the airport, and I tried to get in touch with my family but couldn't get through on my cell phone. Everyone was panicked, very hectic. We found out more in Cleveland. It was all we talked about at our team dinner that night. And the Boston Marathon bombing was on our minds for the remainder of the season. We felt a responsibility to do something special for the city. We knew, from that moment on, that we were playing for something far bigger than our team.

That's what was so special about the whole championship. The Red Sox had won other World Series, but Jonny Gomes said it best: We didn't win a championship for the Boston Red Sox. We won a championship for Boston. And it wasn't even just for Boston: It was a northeastern championship.

We tried to go out on a daily basis and just give it our all. After we returned from a three-game road trip to Cleveland, our home game against Kansas City on Friday, April 19 was postponed as authorities searched for the bombers, who turned out to be Chechen brothers Dzhokhar and Tamerlan Tsarnaev. We were locked down in our apartment next to Fenway Park for the day, and nobody could leave. We went up to the rooftop and ate pizza and watched the news for updates. Many first responders walked into our clubhouse the next day and they were beaten down. They were tired. They had not slept in probably three or four days, and I saw the wear and tear. And it just hit home. They were happy to see us, and that was humbling as a player. We get paid a lot of money to play a game, and our nurses, firefighters, and police officers don't get the recognition and the pay that they should. But here were these people wanting to shake our hands.

When we returned to Fenway Park for Saturday's game, emergency personnel were honored and they played Jeff Buckley's "Hallelujah" during a pregame ceremony. And David Ortiz, of course, took the microphone and shouted a line that became an emotional anthem for Boston: "This is our fucking city!" Everyone came together. It still gives me chills thinking about it today.

We visited hospitals and those visits brightened people's day. You wouldn't believe how happy people were that we came and signed some baseballs and brought them some autographs; some of them had lost limbs. People gave us standing ovations when we walked in. They're laughing and joking with us, and I am just so—I'm a blip on the map. I'm a redneck from Tallahassee. They were the ones who ran toward the injured next to where the bomb exploded. I can't say that I would've done that. You can't fake courage like that.

. . . .

DAVID'S iPHONE JOURNAL
3/6/16

Was nice to get a hit today. Saw the ball good. Missed a few blocks that cost us some runs. Need to work on that! Just got home from Jake's surprise 30th birthday party, it was a blast! Guys told stories and wives chatted. Seeing all the wives made me miss my wife. The boys made fun of me for yelling at Lester! Hahaha, I am an asshole when I play!! It was good to know Adam Warren and a few new guys. The Motte family was there. Always great to see them. Got tomorrow off. We have a split-squad game. Going to go in and work out and then come home.

. . . .

I learned how to win in Boston in 2013. I was obsessed with winning. And, in large part, it was because of the collection of talented players and strong personalities we had. And the season also demonstrated how everything came together to make it so special. We know how the 2014 season ended, right?

Even with the same manager and many of the same players from 2013, we finished last in the American League East to become the first defending champions to finish last in their division the next season since the Florida Marlins in 1998. We also took it a step further in 2014. We were the first major-league team to finish last in one season (2012), win the World Series the next (2013), and finish last again the following year (2014). It was an up-and-down journey in Boston in my two years—I played in 86 games combined—but 2013 is a year I will always cherish because of those guys.

Second baseman Dustin Pedroia gets it. He never shuts off. Ever. I fired him a text message one night around 2 a.m. during the 2013 season. I couldn't sleep and was watching ESPN. I figured Dustin was asleep and wouldn't see the text until the morning. Dustin is the best second baseman I have seen when it comes to defending the push bunt. He's the best at coming forward. So I fired him a text like, "Hey man, you're a stud. You're the best in the game at coming forward." I wanted to compliment him. Well, I get a return text immediately. He was like, "Yeah, yeah, I'll show you the awards tomorrow. Get some rest, we've got a game to win. You're catching tomorrow." That's Dustin. He was saying he knows he's good, he doesn't need me to pump him up. He just needs me to shut up and take care of my catching.

I talked to Hyla all the time about Jonny Gomes. He's just a really unique guy as far as his career path and life story, and his mental side of life, really. He's so arrogant about the fact that he knows exactly what he's going to do. He's like, "I knew I was going to hit a walk-off right there; you didn't?" I'm a guy who plans for the worst so I'm never disappointed. I try not to get disappointed so when things do happen, I am excited. I am fired up. Jonny's the other way around. He knows he's about to do it, and when he does, he gets excited. His approach made me better as a player.

Ryan Dempster was funny in a cocky way. Ryan, Jonny, and myself had spent time in organizations that were decidedly not the Red Sox. The amenities were not the same. With the Sox, we traveled on planes that had a smorgasbord of food, drinks, snacks—healthy, nonhealthy, whatever you wanted. They were family flights and they even had Chick-fil-A kids' meals on them. It was just over the top. Dempsey made fun of it, like, "I'm tired of these Doritos, I want better chips on my flight." He said it jokingly but it was almost like, "Yeah, cater to us because we're going to win the whole thing. We're fixing to nail this. Go ahead and give us whatever we want." The mindset never failed to make me laugh.

Dempster was a good glue piece. He got along with everyone. He can hold a room in a heartbeat. We had one incident on a bus ride—I think we were in New York—where it got a little hairy. Dempster had started to rile the guys, but it was hilarious the way he went about it. We both got off the bus and he looked at me and

I said, "Attaboy." He just started laughing because that was his way of getting everyone going. As a team, we never lost more than three games in a row that season. That's amazing. Some people lose sight of that.

Pitcher Jake Peavy was traded to the Red Sox in July 2013 from the Chicago White Sox. Jake and I had played together in San Diego a few years earlier, in 2005. Jake had been in Boston probably around ten days and he goes, "Rossy, I have never seen anything like this. It's so different. Every day somebody mentions winning the World Series. Every day somebody in this locker room mentions it." I laughed and said, "Bro, it's become just a natural thing." We expected to win.

I remember once when we landed in Cleveland and were going to a team dinner. We had a "show dinner" that night. Steak, lobster, the whole works. That's what we called it, "show dinner." The player who made the most money paid for it. We piled into a cab at the hotel—I think it was me, Dempster, and Lester in the backseat. Pedroia was in the front. The cabbie pulled out and almost immediately he slammed on the brakes. Dustin is dramatic about flying, travel, and everything, and he had this dead straight-face look. He said, "Hey, man, careful, careful. You have the 2013 World Series champs in this car." I lost it. I was laughing my head off. Dustin was dead serious with this driver. The driver didn't speak very good English and I am sure he didn't even understand what Dustin said. But that's what I mean. We talked like that the entire 2013 season. And everyone jumped on board. It was contagious.

We also ragged manager John Farrell and the coaches. Nobody was safe on the team, and I think that was the greatest thing about that Red Sox team. On the best teams I played for, you could beat each other up in a good way. That allowed you to play freely. If I popped up, somebody the next day might say, "Nice job on that pop-up." The mindset: everybody knows you are doing your best, so let's make fun of the bad times.

One game we were scrapping for hits against pitcher Bud Norris and the Houston Astros. Farrell had given Dustin the sign for a hit-and-run against Norris. Dustin popped up and he came back into the dugout pissed. But he was not going to show up anybody. The next day he was in the locker room and passed John. And Dustin said, "[Expletive] Bud Norris." And we all laughed. He said, "I am a three-hole hitter for the Sox, and you give me a hit-and-run against Bud [expletive] Norris." Everyone lost it, including John. It was one of those things where Dustin was telling us, "Hey, man, I am going to rake that guy." I always asked Dustin how he was doing. He would always respond something to the effect of, "How am I? How do you think I am, David? I am a career .303 hitter. I've got a gorgeous wife, two kids, and I have a $170 million contract. How the [expletive] do you think I am." I love that guy!

There was so much camaraderie on that team. It's like the beards. I had a zigzag line shaved into the back of my head thanks to Big Papi. I was thirty-six years old! We just had a group of guys who bought into whatever was going on. If someone said, "Hey, I'm going to paint my fingernails today for a week, let's do it," everybody was on board, let's go. We just had that type of group.

The beards started in spring training. Napoli came to me and said he and Gomes were growing beards and I should join them. He said it would be awesome. So I grew mine out with him and, after a while, everyone's beards were thick and nasty. When I was sent home in August with the concussion, I couldn't go anywhere. And my beard was itching, just a mess. Hyla said, "Why don't you shave it?" I couldn't. I knew those guys wouldn't let me back in the locker room.

The beard tug started when I went to Napoli and told him that the next time he hit a home run, I was going to pull the shit out of his beard. It hurts like hell when somebody tugs on your beard. I told him he'd be so happy he wouldn't care. He hit a home run and I just pulled the shit out of it. It went crazy. Everyone started to do it. It was just another sign of our closeness. It didn't matter who you were, you were buying in. Guys who could barely grow beards, or could only grow ugly beards, had them, too.

We had so many cool stories that year, just very human stories. If you watch the World Series film from 2013, you can see Dempster and Peavy standing along the line before the national anthem one game and they are saying, "Boy, we are in the World Series." Laughing, like can you believe this? How cool is this? These are guys who have played professional baseball fifteen, sixteen years and they are in awe of the moment. I cherished those moments, too. The way they enjoyed the moment stood out to me, and I've tried to bring that enjoyment to the rest of my career.

In Game Five of the Series against the Cardinals, I started at catcher for the Sox. Starting pitcher Jon Lester and Koji Uehara were great on the mound in the 3–1 win that give us a three-games-to-two lead. I also had the game-winning hit on an RBI ground-rule double off Cardinals starter Adam Wainwright in the two-run seventh inning. Following the game, I was brought into the media room and stood behind a podium that usually was reserved for the marquee players, not for backup catchers.

Everyone wanted to talk about my big hit. At the press conference, everybody asked how was it, the hit. I was like, "The hit was great, but I'm playing in the World Series. Do you understand how cool this is? I'm at the podium talking to you guys." I told them I wasn't going anywhere. They could've asked me questions for four hours and I would've sat there and answered every one of them.

◇

After we won the World Series, we had a couple of days to decompress. I went to Fenway and into the locker room—we had a bunch of items to autograph—and Ben Cherington was there. I asked if we could talk. He said yes so we went into John Farrell's office. I said, "Hey, I haven't asked this all year and I have heard different things, but I'd like to know why you wanted me. Why was I a priority? What did you see in me?" I knew what I brought to the table, I knew the Red Sox recognized that, but I asked Ben how he saw it. I know what I brought to teams wasn't always on paper. You either had to watch me play or hear from other players what I bring to a team.

Ben said there were two things they looked at when they signed me. He said the first was the pitching staff. It meant a great deal to the organization but it had struggled in 2012. Ben felt there were a couple of different ways to fix it. The Red Sox could get new pitchers, and they didn't want to do that. Ben felt the talent was there and most of the pitchers were under contract, heavy contracts, and it would be difficult to move players.

When Farrell came in, he brought in a new pitching coach, Juan Nieves, and they needed another catcher. Ben explained there are two primary ways to win games—score a bunch or don't allow many runs. He said the organization felt I was on that end of the equation, that I didn't allow many runs. Ben said the organization did its research and found out a number of things, including what kind of person I was. They did their research and my name came up and when John came here, they asked him, "Would you like to have David Ross?" According to Ben, John had jumped out of his seat and said he'd love to have me.

All I could say was, "Wow."

CHAPTER 8

CONTRERAS OFF THE WALL

9:14 P.M.

Game Tied, 1–1

Joe Maddon went with the same starting lineup in Game Seven that won him Game Six a day earlier.

Who could blame him, right? We beat Cleveland 9–3 in Game Six, propelled by 13 hits and 3 home runs. That meant twenty-four-year-old rookie Willson Contreras would catch starter Kyle Hendricks in what had shaped up to be one of the most anticipated games in Major League Baseball history. I know the media was speculating I might start behind the plate because of my experience, combined with the fact that it was literally my last game.

But I already knew my role for Game Seven. Maddon told me the night before that I'd probably play since it was his intention to bring in relief pitcher Jon Lester if needed. That was my focus and preparation. I also knew Willson was prepared to handle the moment, and it was a big one for him: His fifth World Series start would tie him with Buster Posey for the most World Series starts for a rookie catcher since Red Hayworth in 1944. (Don't you love crazy baseball statistics?)

I said it to the media and anybody else who would listen: Willson is a phenomenal talent. He was such a huge part of our team from the moment he was promoted on June 17, from Triple-A Iowa. I knew in spring training, when I saw his skills firsthand, that if we were going to win a championship, he was going to be a big part of making it happen. The day after he was called up to the majors we were playing the Pittsburgh Pirates at Wrigley Field. Willson was inserted into the game to catch the ninth inning of our 6–0 win and received a standing ovation in his debut. Cubs fans understood, too: This guy meant a lot to the present and future of the ball club. Two days later, in a 10–5 victory over the Pirates, he pinch-hit for Hendricks in the sixth inning and received another standing ovation. On the first pitch he saw from A. J. Schugel—a high changeup—he banged a two-run home run over the right-center outfield wall. It was the first pitch he had seen in the major leagues! I mean, who does that?

Willson's a great player. Anybody who followed our team on a day-to-day basis saw it, too. He's big, strong, and athletic at six-foot-one and 212 pounds. A right-handed batter with pop. He's got an absolute cannon for an arm. He has great energy and is fearless. He wanted to improve and he worked hard at it. His catching and game-calling skills improved tremendously over the 2016 season.

Starting Willson for Game Seven was a careful decision on Joe's part. And a good one: With the game tied 1–1 in the fourth inning of Game Seven, he came up big.

Kris Bryant led off the inning and worked an eight-pitch at-bat against Indians starter Corey Kluber before he singled to left field.

Kluber plunked Anthony Rizzo in the right shoulder to put run-ners on first and second base with no outs for Ben Zobrist. Zobrist hit into a ground-ball fielder's choice, forcing out Rizzo at second base and advancing Bryant to third.

Kris then made a great read on Addison Russell's shallow pop-up to center fielder Rajai Davis, breaking for home as Davis caught the ball and sliding under the tag of Roberto Perez to break the tie.

Then Willson came to the plate.

With two outs, he hung back on a 2-2 curveball and smacked it into deep center, over the head of Davis to extend our lead to 3–1.

Willson might have been 1-for-17 heading into Game Seven but he was not intimidated by how big the moment was. He grinds every at-bat and has a great two-strike approach. He wears his emo-tions on his sleeve, and it was fun to watch his reaction when he reached second base after his double. He pounded his chest and blew a kiss to the sky. He pointed to us in the first base dugout, clenched, and churned his fists like pistons.

I loved it.

◇

Willson Contreras was signed by the Cubs as a free agent in July 2009 out of his native Venezuela. He's a versatile guy who played just about every position in the minor leagues—catcher, first base, second base, third base, left field, and right field. He had a breakout year in 2015, when he was named the Cubs' Minor League Player of the Year after batting .333 with eight home runs. That's when he really positioned himself on the Cubs' big-league radar as a catcher.

When I arrived at spring training in February 2016 in Mesa, Arizona, I could tell Willson would be the future catcher for years to come, sooner or later. I was hoping later. I knew going into my last year that if my performance started suffering, then I was probably out the door, whenever that time was. Preferably, of course, that would be the end of the season.

Because I knew it was my last season, I took care to give Willson all the support and knowledge I could during spring training. That's what teammates do for one another. I don't want in any way to appear as if I'm taking any of the credit for Willson's skills. The guy has gifts.

When pitchers and catchers reported to spring training, Willson was basically third in line behind Miguel Montero and myself. In spring training, it's usually the starter, the backup, and then the minor-league guys rotating in during drills. They are included in the mix. Since Contreras hails from Venezuela just like Miggy (Montero), they had a natural bond. But I watched and tried to help out as best I could. I knew he would be promoted at some point during the season to give the team a boost.

Willson didn't know me, and I really didn't know him, which meant that I needed to make the extra effort to connect with him. That's not always the way it has been in baseball, especially with rookies. Back when I was coming up in the Los Angeles Dodgers organization, the rookies got a lot more heat. Sometimes it was playful, but sometimes it was a little more like hazing. Sometimes it stemmed out of jealousy—some guy was worried you were going to take his job. I never wanted anyone to feel that way because I understand how bad that made me feel. It made me want to compete against that guy, and I didn't like that feeling of competing against a teammate.

So I always kept that in mind, especially when I dealt with catchers. I may have gotten on some rookies, but I never got on a rookie catcher, because I didn't want to be misconstrued on what my intentions were. I left that for other guys, other veterans. I was there to be positive, so that's how I approached our 2016 spring training with Willson. If I saw something that needed to be corrected, I tried to be positive about the way I presented it.

The only thing Willson really had to work on when he got to the major leagues was his game calling. That is one of those skills you improve from being on the job. You can't really teach it. Young catchers have to go out there and play the game. They have to learn the pitchers and learn how the league works and how to manage a big-league lineup for nine innings.

When you see a guy with Willson's talent, it is pretty obvious he is going to be in the big leagues sooner rather than later. So I tried to help out wherever I could. Luckily for me, Willson is a polite guy. He respected me, and he respected the game. It was refreshing to see a young player who treated you as he wanted to be treated, and didn't act like the arrogant, cocky upstart who thought he knew it all. Willson's not that kind of guy at all.

．．．．．．．．．．．．．．．．

DAVID'S iPHONE JOURNAL
3/25/16

Went to Octane with Huddy, Peav, and their kids last night. We had a blast. Great to see Huddy happy. Seems he is enjoying retirement. Great day today at camp! Joe brought in two black bear clubs that we got to hold. Was cool holding and playing with them. Good swings the last few days. Catching feels good, too. Need to stay on top of my workouts. I feel strong in the legs. Miss my family. They have a bunch of things going on for Easter. Always stinks to miss the big Easter egg hunt at Lorna's.

. . . .

The catcher's life is unique in baseball. When people think of the great players in baseball history, most are position players or pitchers. There have been some amazing catchers over the years, like Johnny Bench and Yogi Berra—and even Yogi might mostly be known for his funny sayings. But he was an amazing catcher, even if most people just don't realize it.

It's true that in MLB history there have been few great all-around players who were catchers. Those guys are few and far between even now. A Buster Posey comes around once every ten years, if we're lucky. I'd also point to Yadier Molina of St. Louis and Brian McCann of Houston as being guys who can really hit, catch, and throw.

Why are there so few all-around great players who catch? One reason is that there's so much that goes into catching. Hitting is its own skill set. Then a catcher has to worry about his team's pitchers and how they are doing. And then a catcher has to study the other team's lineup, understand his opponents' strengths and weaknesses at the plate, and call the game accordingly. You might not realize it sitting at home watching a game on TV, but so much goes into choosing what pitch gets thrown to a given hitter.

Managing the lineup is a critical part of the catcher's job. You always have to be thinking on your feet. Say Albert Pujols is coming to the plate. Okay, I am not going to let Albert Pujols beat us, but after Albert Pujols in the lineup is Matt Holiday. How do I get around Albert Pujols and still have to pitch to Matt Holiday? And who is after Matt Holiday in the lineup? Do we walk Matt Holiday with two outs? You have to manage the lineup and the game situation and what matchup works best for your pitcher. It's a cat-and-mouse game. For instance, when Albert came to the plate, I might try to steal a first-pitch strike with a fastball. If I got the strike, I could expand the strike zone to put more pressure on him by throwing off-speed pitches an inch or two off the plate. If we fell behind 2-and-0, I might decide to go ahead and walk him on pitches to set up his next at-bat.

From a strategic standpoint, there's not a more important position on the field than catcher. And that's my favorite thing about the role. It's a chess match. The batter knows what my pitcher has, but he doesn't know how we plan to get him out. Are we going to pound him inside? Are we going to work outside the strike zone to see if he chases outside the zone? Are we going to attack him because he's the batter we want to get out? One mistake in your calculations could cost you the game.

I always sat down with my starting pitcher before every game and to go over our opponent's lineup: the guys we should get out, the guys who are the tough outs, and the guy we don't want to beat us. We would discuss where a walk might be just as good as an out. If a guy had big-time power and thus a chance to change the game in a swing, we might not want to deal with him.

The pitcher and catcher, as a pair, are the equivalent of the quarterback in football, or perhaps the quarterback plus the offensive coordinator. They work together and manage the game. The pitcher has all the pressure on him. The catcher, the guy behind the curtain, is calling the plays. But the catcher can't do much if the guy behind the mound isn't any good. If all my pitcher can do is throw 91 mph meatballs down the middle, we won't be sitting pretty. But if a pitcher has control and a deep arsenal of pitches, the game calling and strategy can be so much fun—and often the key to winning the game.

Take Tim Hudson with his heavy sinker. He sinks hitters in and sliders away. You look at other pitchers like him, like Roy Halladay, who is going to use sinkers on both sides of the plate. You kind of knew how those guys wanted to pitch you. They could throw strikes to both sides of the plate and make the ball go two different directions—imagine an X across the top of the plate. When I was batting, I always had to try to guess what side of the plate the pitch was headed—and hope I guessed right. It was like a game inside the game.

When I started my career with the Dodgers, I learned a lot from our catching instructors. Guys like Del Crandall and Rick Dempsey, a guy who played twenty-four years in the major leagues. Rick helped me change my catcher's crouch from knees in to knees out—it was the stance I used for the rest of my career. At six foot two and 230 pounds, I made myself a bigger target for our pitchers with my knees out.

Another important influence in my time at the Dodgers was catcher Paul Lo Duca. He was a supernice guy who made me feel welcomed. Paul helped me understand how to interact with pitchers. Paul always hung out with them. And I also grew to love sitting with pitchers and getting to know their personalities and what they talked and thought about. Paul even ran our pitchers' meetings, sharing his observations about every hitter on the opposing team. It was very impressive, and it was instrumental in my own growth as a game caller behind the plate.

◇

When Contreras was promoted to the big-league team and arrived at Wrigley Field on Thursday, June 16, I gave him a big hug and announced the prodigy had arrived. Miggy Montero told the *Chicago Tribune*, "We're on our way out, man," referring to both himself and me. "He's on the way in. We're happy for him, of course."

Miggy was right. I was happy for Willson. He was part of a young Cubs nucleus that included players like third baseman Kris Bryant, first baseman Anthony Rizzo, shortstop Addison Russell, infielder Javier Baez, and outfielder/catcher Kyle Schwarber.

Cubs president Theo Epstein gave me a heads-up a few days earlier about Willson's promotion. He explained the plan and shared what management wanted to do with Willson. It wasn't something he had to do, but it showed the front office cared and that they understood the inner workings of the clubhouse. That is extremely important. You can be a better player, a better teammate, a better person if you have a clear understanding of your role.

If plans are kept secretive and roles undefined, when a new guy arrives you might begin to wonder where you fit in. It's difficult to head to work when you don't know where you stack up in your organization's plans. It might make you anxious. If something goes wrong, you may be quick to lash out and want to blame others because you're frustrated.

Theo and Joe and the rest of the Cubs management understand those things. The Cubs communicate a lot better than even Boston did when I was in the Red Sox organization (2013–14), and they had been the best I had experienced.

Willson had earned the promotion—he batted .350 with 9 home runs, 43 RBIs, and 16 doubles in 54 games at Triple-A Iowa. Most important, we needed him in the big leagues since we were thin at catcher due to injuries. Miggy missed time when he tweaked his back. Schwarber, a double talent in left field and at catcher, played in the opening two games of the season before he tore the ACL and LCL in his left knee in an outfield collision with center fielder Dexter Fowler. Tim Federowicz was promoted from Triple-A Iowa when Miggy went down. And here I was, the old guy, on pace to have my most plate appearances in nine seasons. Could I last the season without sustaining a major injury? In early July, just before the All-Star break, I went on the seven-day disabled list because of concussion-like symptoms after I took a foul tip off the face mask in a game against the Reds.

That was the calculus for the front office. Willson probably caught a little more than the brass expected right off the bat, but he stepped up to the challenge. He fit right into the lineup and had great at-bats, right from the start. The number-one rule for a catcher is to show he cares about the pitching staff and not just about himself. I saw quickly that Willson was really passionate about winning and tried to get the most out of his pitchers. He has leadership qualities.

This is a fact: Willson was a better player than I was. His athleticism was astonishing. I had to check any pride and selfishness and think about what was best for the team. I knew the best way I could help the team was talking to him, just to give a little bit of veteran advice at the right times. The only thing I could control was how I treated him and everyone else on the team.

. . . .

DAVID'S iPHONE JOURNAL
4/1/16

April Fools! Leaving Vegas for Anaheim. Off tomorrow, exhibition Sunday, and then opening day. It has been one of my favorite spring trainings. Went 3 for 3 my last game with all doubles. Starting to prepare for my first start on Tuesday. Getting butterflies. Vegas was fun. Played hungover yesterday. It has been a while since I did that. My first show suite was amazing. Had a two bedroom on top floor with Rizz. Amazing view. We have a great group of guys and everyone is ready to get this thing started.

. . . .

Willson said early on that he wanted to absorb everything he could from Miggy and myself. And he was receptive in that regard.

I remember we played Seattle in late July 2016 at Wrigley Field, and Willson was behind the plate. Nelson Cruz was up early in the game with two outs, a base open, and in a fastball count. But Willson tried to flip a breaking ball or a changeup in to steal a strike— it's called pitching backward when a pitcher relies on his secondary pitches rather than his fastball in a fastball count. It was an unaggressive pitch. Cruz is a veteran, middle-of-the-order right-handed hitter and those guys get pitched backward a lot. They understand the game. And Nelson hammered the pitch into left-center field.

When a player has been around as long as Cruz has, he understands the pitcher is probably not going to give in to him. Especially if there's a left-handed batter on deck and a left-handed pitcher on the mound, as in this situation. As a catcher, you are looking for the better matchup behind Cruz. You have to understand who is at the plate and what they might be thinking. Don't give in to this guy, you've got a better matchup on deck. It's a better situation, play the percentages.

After Cruz socked his hit, I knew I wanted to talk to Willson about that situation and how he handled it. You don't want to do it the moment he walks into the dugout, though. You don't want to be second-guessing him right away. It is so easy to second-guess others because when something doesn't work out, you are always going to be like, "Dang, you should have gone with a slider or a fastball, or vice versa." I don't believe in that. I just tried to tell Willson what I'd learned from my experiences.

So I waited a few innings and he was near me, so I said, "Hey, Willie, come here real quick." I asked him about the pitch to Cruz and he said it was a breaking ball. I asked if he was trying to pitch around Cruz, and he said yes, that "I didn't want to give in to that guy." I said okay, here's what I have learned. I told him I understood exactly what he was thinking. But I did it in a way like, "Listen, I understand what you're thinking and it's not wrong." I told him he wasn't wrong but I shared what in my experience might work better. Cruz probably gets pitched around a lot, especially with a base open, and might have been looking for something soft. In my experience, pitchers try to be too careful when pitching around guys and don't have great control of their off-speed pitches. I told Willson to use the fastball to extreme sides of the plate. Pitchers usually have better command of that pitch.

If I had marched out to him and said, "Well, you should have done this," that wouldn't have helped anybody. It's all about saying, "Hey, I can relate to what was going on in that count. Let me tell you what I have learned over the years." Plus, game calling is the easiest area to second-guess when things don't work out, and you don't want it to feel like you're down on them, or you're being negative. I always tried to be positive, to present feedback in terms of mistakes that I've made in my own career. Don't make the same mistakes I made!

The other thing about giving feedback is that you don't do it all day, every day. It's got to be in small doses at the right moment. That way you won't make someone defensive and you'll build trust. After a while you might find the guy in the dugout asking questions unprompted.

These teaching spots happened a lot in my relationship with Kyle Schwarber, starting when he was called up as a rookie in 2015. Around the time Kyle was starting to catch there was a game where we were getting our brains beat out. Absolutely getting killed. I was starting to get to know Kyle and building that relationship. He walked down the dugout and asked, "What do you got?" It was one of those moments: he came to me and we had that trust so I was honest with him.

I said, "Man, honestly, your body language behind the plate looks like we're getting beat. Everybody is looking at you; you're the leader back there. Your body language is telling me we're down twenty runs. I understand we're getting hammered, but everybody is looking at you. What your body language and your energy level presents—well, that's how we're going to play."

It's a fact. If a player is down and he's dragging, the impression he gives is, "Oh, this game is over." So everyone is going to act accordingly and the feeling becomes contagious. What I tried to explain to Kyle in that quick conversation was to make sure his body language was consistent with how he *wanted* to play, not what the score was.

I always tried to keep negative thoughts to myself. Baseball is a hard game. And when you are sitting on the bench and have no control over what is going on, it is easy to get frustrated because you can't affect the immediate outcome. But that mindset is losing baseball. A winning team doesn't have negative players sitting on the bench saying they would have done things differently. Keeping your negative thoughts to yourself is just as important as sharing something positive.

That's why being around Willson was so much fun. He wasn't afraid to make a mistake. He wanted to learn. He made adjustments. He made progress in every area. He had high expectations, just like me and everyone else within the organization. He batted .282 with 12 home runs and started at catcher in 41 games—on a team that carried three catchers into the postseason.

And in Game Seven of the World Series in Cleveland, Willson came up big in the fourth inning with his two-out double. It gave us a 3–1 lead and some breathing room.

CHAPTER 9

JUST CONTINUE TO BREATHE

9:30 P.M.

Cubs Lead, 5–1

Thirty minutes before Game Seven, MLB Network producer Danny Field asked if I would wear a live mic for the game. Danny has helped produce Major League Baseball's World Series documentaries over the years and is really a good guy.

I got to know him in 2013, when I was with the Boston Red Sox and we won the World Series over the St. Louis Cardinals. I had worn a live mic before in other games during my career, and I never minded it. You really kind of forget it is there. Plus, I trusted that Danny would not embarrass me or the team—they promised to edit the tape before it was aired. So I said okay.

In the top of the fifth, the network caught a wired-up exchange between first baseman Anthony Rizzo and myself and aired it as part of its "Sounds of the Game" segment during the game broadcast. That allowed viewers at home to listen in on our conversation (a few minutes after it occurred) in the dugout.

Second baseman Javier Baez had just homered to right-center field on the first pitch of the inning off Cleveland starter Corey Kluber. Baez's home run extended our lead to 4–1. Rizzo, with his left arm draped over my left shoulder as I stood in front of the dugout railing, told me he was an "emotional wreck" and in a "glass case of emotions right now." It probably was the first time a professional player quoted the 2004 movie *Anchorman* during a World Series—Vince Vaughn was one of the stars of that movie and had visited our clubhouse during the 2016 season—but Anthony was being honest about the moment.

Here's the full exchange:

ROSS: Talk to me.

RIZZO: I can't control myself right now. I'm trying my best.

ROSS: It's understandably so, buddy.

RIZZO: I'm emotional.

ROSS: I hear you.

RIZZO: I'm an emotional wreck.

ROSS: It's only going to get worse. Just continue to breathe. That's all you do, buddy. That's all you can do. It's only going to get worse.

RIZZO: I'm in a glass case of emotion right now.

ROSS: Yeah. Yeah. Wait until the ninth with this three-run lead.

That three-run lead turned into a four-run lead later in the fifth inning, thanks to Rizzo.

The Indians replaced Kluber with left-handed reliever Andrew Miller following Baez's home run. Kluber threw 57 pitches, 36 for strikes, but didn't have strikeouts, compared to the 15 he fanned in his first two starts of the Series.

Dexter Fowler greeted Miller with a 1-2 single to left field past a diving Francisco Lindor at shortstop. Kyle Schwarber grounded into a 6-4-3 double play, but Kris Bryant followed with a great at-bat. He drew a walk on the ninth pitch of his at-bat that saw Andrew throw six consecutive sliders.

That brought up the "emotional" Rizzo. Despite the volcano of feelings inside him, Rizzo, a left-handed hitter, worked a 1-2 count before lashing a single to right field. Kris took off on the pitch and scored easily from first. Rizzo advanced to second on the throw to home plate. Ben Zobrist then hit a long fly ball into center field and Rajai Davis made a running catch a few steps in front of the wall for the third out.

. . . .

DAVID'S iPHONE JOURNAL
4/18/16

Opening day was not as cool as I was hoping for. Was just happy to get the season started. We played well, and I had a good game the second game. Is always nice to get that first hit out of the way. Was cool to start my last season at the same place I got called up and got my first at-bat. Got a cool story about Bubba, the clubhouse manager in Anaheim. He didn't make guys who made their debut with him pay dues. But you had to sign his debut ball and date it. He still had the ball and had me sign the sweet spot for my last year. What a great guy! We had an off day back in Arizona yesterday and beat the Dbacks tonight. We may have lost Schwarber. He got tangled with Dex in the outfield. So I am catching Hammel tomorrow. Should be fun. Looking forward to getting home and seeing my family. Can't wait to see Wrigley rocking. Miss my kids and wife bad. Need some family time.

• • • • • • • • • • • • • • • •

Rizzo was selected by the Boston Red Sox in the sixth round of the 2007 MLB draft out of Stoneman-Douglas High in Parkland, Florida. Theo Epstein, general manager and executive vice president of the Red Sox, traded Rizzo to San Diego in 2010—but with the promise he'd see him again. Anthony made his major-league debut on June 9, 2011, against the Washington Nationals. But, as promised, Epstein, who had left the Red Sox for the Cubs in 2011, traded for Rizzo in January 2012. He's been a fixture in Chicago ever since because of his incredible talent and personality.

I watched Anthony Rizzo as closely as I watched anybody when I sat on the bench. I expected a lot out of him. He is my friend. I know what he's capable of, and I was probably hard on him because

I can't even imagine what he's ultimately capable of as a player. He was consistently one of our best at-bats. His two-strike approach is the best I have seen in my career.

In our last regular-season game of 2016, however, against the Cincinnati Reds at Wrigley, Rizzo didn't go to his two-strike approach when he led off the bottom of the eighth inning against Reds reliever Blake Wood. We led 3–2. Rizzo fell behind in the count 0-2. On the fourth pitch of the at-bat, he strikes out swinging. It was his normal swing, one without any of the adjustments he normally made with two strikes. He didn't choke up on the bat. He still used his usual high leg kick, and he didn't move on top of the plate to better see outside pitches.

I noticed all this from the bench. I had planned to give him a great big bear hug and congratulate him on a great season after his at-bat—he was the first Cubs player in franchise history to hit thirty-plus home runs over three consecutive seasons. But I probably didn't give him enough time to collect his thoughts when he returned to the dugout. He was at the bat rack, taking off his gloves, when he saw me walking toward him. He looked at me and said, "What!? What!? I didn't want to go to my two-strike approach."

I walked up to him and, without any emotion on my face, hugged him and said, "Hey, man, congratulations on a great year." He was real quiet, and I just walked back down the dugout and sat on the bench. A few seconds later, Anthony walked down and said, "Hey, man. Sorry." He didn't have to apologize. But he knew what he did, and he knew that I knew what he did. He knew that I was watching him, too. I told him, "Don't apologize to me, bro. It's your career, not mine."

I told the truth to Anthony and I was on him because I love him. He is the guy everyone is watching. He sets the tone for our team. Veterans don't talk to guys they don't care about. I learned that early in baseball. Young players would wonder, Why is this dude always on me? Veterans give younger players a hard time when they like them. When veterans are not talking to you, watch out. They probably don't like the way you are acting.

With Rizzo it was like a big brother–little brother relationship—he's twelve years younger than me. But I rode his ass when I needed to. On the afternoon of Thursday, September 17, 2015, we were playing in Pittsburgh and had the bases loaded with no outs against Pirates right-handed starter Charlie Morton. Dexter Fowler singled, Kyle Schwarber singled, and Chris Coughlan reached on a fielding error to open the game. Rizzo, in the cleanup hole, was up. With a 1-1 count, Anthony rolled over a pitch and hit into 4-6-3 double play.

I was always on Anthony about having a quality at-bat. I know I wasn't a great hitter, so criticizing Rizzo or a Kris Bryant on their batting was a little bit out of my league. But I had watched how the great ones worked their at-bats, and I also knew when there was a teachable moment. And that swing was a teachable moment. We had Morton on the ropes in the first inning, but I thought, "This dude [Rizzo] didn't come to play." I watched Anthony like a hawk and I was on the bench pissed, fuming. A few innings later he asked me what I thought, and I just laid into him. I said, "You want the truth?"

And he said, "Yeah." Anthony's such a nice kid, but I let him have it.

"You're telling me Charlie Morton gets you to roll over on the first pitch? I watched your at-bat. You're not locked in today."

I couldn't believe he didn't punch me in the face after that! Well, later, in the fifth inning, Anthony unloaded on Morton and smacked a two-run home run to erase a one-run deficit. As soon as Anthony hit it, he looked directly at me and pointed in the dugout like, "Fuck you."

When he came in the dugout, he was in my face. I told him that if he needed me to yell at him every game to make him better, I'd yell at him every day. That was the kind of relationship we had. We were honest with each other, and we got really close.

Look what he achieved in 2016. He won his first Gold Glove (superior fielding) and Silver Slugger (best offensive player at each position) awards. He finished in the top five of the National League MVP voting after hitting .292 with 32 home runs and a career-high 109 RBIs. (Cubs third baseman Kris Bryant was the runaway MVP pick with 29 of a possible 30 first-place votes, with the only other vote putting him in second place.)

I told Tom Verducci of *Sports Illustrated* for a July 2016 story he did on Anthony that Rizzo was "probably the most important player we have on our team," and I meant it. It wasn't just his skills on the field, it was also his attitude. "Every time you're around him, whether you're on the field or out to dinner or any place, he wants everybody to have a good time," I told Tom. "He's more worried about everybody else and puts himself second. Whether it's his at-bats, batting practice or anything, he's quick to take a backseat to others. That's unusual for a superstar."

Jonny Gomes, one of my good friends and a teammate of mine on the 2013 Boston Red Sox, once called me a chameleon because I knew how to fit in any situation. He said I could make friends in a room full of strangers. It was something I had to do all my life, but I always felt comfortable in my surroundings. You adapted or you got left behind, right? I thought the same thing of Anthony. He was a chameleon. He kept tabs on everyone on the Cubs team during my two seasons. If you didn't have family in town, he'd fire out a text inviting you to dinner. He wanted to make sure everyone was included. He was the heart of our team.

• • • • • • • • • • • • • • • •

DAVID'S iPHONE JOURNAL
4/10/16

First road trip in the books. The boys went 5-1 and had a chance to win the one loss. Jake went deep in his second start against Arizona. Lester and Lack have to buy him a watch per their bet for the first pitcher to hit a homer. Mark Grace and the Dbacks did a nice video for me. Going to send him a thank you when they come to see our place. We did lose Schwarber for the year with a knee injury. That really sucks. Super excited about the home opener. Keep thinking it's going to be like the playoffs last year. It was so electric. I get to catch Jon, which is really cool too. Last home opener may be the best one since getting my ring in Boston. I AM SO EXCITED TO SEE MY FAMILY!! It has been way too long. Kids are changing fast. Pretty sure wife could use a break, haha.

• • • • • • • • • • • • • • • •

Rizzo is a special dude. Most know he beat cancer, too. In May 2008 he was diagnosed with Hodgkin's lymphoma. He went through chemotherapy for six months, and in November 2008, his doctors told him "he could live a normal life." He hasn't stopped living, either. We connected immediately and I know the guy knows how to have fun. Sometimes at my expense, too.

It all started because of my own self-deprecation when it came to admitting how old I was. I made fun of myself a lot, especially in 2015, when I signed with the Cubs and was the team's clear elder statesman at thirty-nine.

One night during spring training in 2016 I was at dinner with Rizzo, Kris Bryant, and a few other guys and we started talking about Instagram, the social media app. I always made fun of them always checking their phones and stuff posted on those sites, mainly because I had no idea how it worked. (Keep in mind, when I started my professional baseball career, people were still using dial-up Internet!) So, Rizzo and K.B. were like, "We're going to start an Instagram account for you." So the very next day we were in the locker room and they showed me an Instagram account dubbed "Grandpa Rossy."

They never called me grandpa, but it was the name they came up with. I joked that the guys were treating me like I had one foot in the grave, but they said they wanted me to feel special. The Instagram account was a fun way to say they cared about me and were going to miss me. They wanted to take some photographs and get some videos of me and have some fun with the account. The first three pictures on the account were one of me posing at a sporting goods store with a Cubs shirt and mitt in one hand, and pants, batting gloves, and knee pads before my "last first day"; another one of Rizzo, Bryant, and me at a Phoenix Suns game; and a black-and-white baseball card of me from when I was with the Los Angeles Dodgers.

Anything those whippersnappers touched was gold. The next thing I knew the "Grandpa Rossy" account had hit 24,000 followers. It was still the first day, February 21. Within a week I couldn't go to a game without being called "Grandpa." People in the stands were like, "Grandpa, Grandpa." John Lackey, a year younger than me at thirty-eight, asked, "Are you going to let them call you grandpa?" But what could I do? The thing had taken on a life of its own.

At one point during spring training, some of the guys presented me with a motorized scooter "to help me get around." "At first, we kind of felt bad calling him grandpa," Bryant acknowledged to a *Chicago Tribune* reporter. "He's like 38 years old. That's pretty young for a normal person. He's enjoyed it."

The younger guys loved it because it got me so much more attention when we were out and about. We'd go to dinner and people would come up and ask for a photo or an autograph. I'd never taken so many pictures or signed so many autographs in my life, including when I'd won the Series with Boston in 2013.

One time a guy yelled across a restaurant, "Hey Grandpa!" when I walked in. The guy had to have been fifteen years older than me. I started looking around like, is this guy talking to me? I'd be out to dinner with Hyla and the kids, and people would ask for pictures. It got so crazy that I had to ask my family if they were okay with me having my photograph taken while we were out. They'd say, "That's fine, Dad, as long as it doesn't take forever."

The "Grandpa Rossy" phenomenon started to get press attention, and eventually the Cubs organization got into the action, too. An official Grandpa Rossy T-shirt was designed and the Cubs started selling them at Wrigley. It was crazy.

The Cubs also produced a series of videos with me to help generate All-Star votes for my teammates. In one, I—as Grandpa

Rossy—use a rotary phone to implore fans to dial "#votecubs" and call in their vote. In another, I encourage them to fax in their votes.

Honestly, I loved it all.

◇

One of my most vivid memories from the Series is what Rizzo did after we fell behind the Indians three games to one. Rizzo wanted to fire up everybody, as well as ease some of the crazy pressure we were all feeling. So in the clubhouse before Game Five at Wrigley Field, Rizzo started playing *Rocky* movie quotes over the speaker system. *Rocky* is, of course, the rags-to-riches 1976 movie that starred Sylvester Stallone as Rocky Balboa, a boxer who overcame long odds to get a shot at the world heavyweight championship. Rizzo also had these other movie speeches on his iPad, like Al Pacino's from *Any Given Sunday.*

Anthony played these speeches as he walked around and beat his chest. Everyone was like, "Oh, it's just Rizzo." When the theme song from *Rocky* came on, he was full-monty theatrics. He ran into the locker room naked, jumped up and down, and shadowboxed his way around the entire room. He kept saying, "It's not how many times you get knocked down, it's how many times you get up." The place erupted; everyone was laughing. But we won Game Five, 3–2.

For Game Six we headed back to Cleveland and Rizzo did the same thing. Naked, jumped up and down, shadowboxed, saying, "It's not how many times you get knocked down, it's how many times you get up." And we won that game, too, 9–3.

So it was a given that the same routine would happen before Game Seven. This time Rizzo ended up on a coffee table in the locker room. Just then one of the players thought he'd be funny and took a can of shoe cleaner and sprayed Rizzo. Rizzo was pissed, but he didn't want to show it so he went straight to the shower and washed off.

After Rizzo had been gone about five minutes, his saying popped into my head: "It's not how many times you get knocked down, it's how many times you get back up." After the spraying incident, the vibe in the locker room had immediately changed, so I walked toward the shower area as Rizzo was toweling off.

"You all right, man?" I asked. He still was pissed and ready to light into the player, but I said, "It's not how many times you get knocked down . . ."

Suddenly he looked up and flashed a grin at me. "You're right, you're right," he said. And then he proceeded to drop his towel and run back into the locker room and start his whole routine again. I could only stand there and laugh.

CHAPTER 10

CALL TO THE BULLPEN

9:52 P.M.

Cubs Lead, 5–1

In the bottom of the fifth inning, starter Kyle Hendricks got the first two outs on a grounder to second from Coco Crisp and a strikeout of Roberto Perez as we led 5–1. But when Kyle walked Carlos Santana, Joe Maddon summoned left-hander Jon Lester, our Game Five starter and winner, from the bullpen.

Of course, Joe's decision raised eyebrows. After our 9–3 victory over Cleveland in Game Six the previous night, Joe told the media Jon was available in relief for Game Seven—with a catch. Joe said he didn't want to bring Lester into a "dirty inning," meaning he wouldn't bring Jon into the game in the middle of the inning.

The reasons behind Joe's strategy weren't a deep secret.

Jon wasn't accustomed to the role. His last relief appearance was nine years earlier, when he was with the Boston Red Sox. Jon entered twice in relief in the 2007 American League Championship

Series against, ironically, the Indians. And Jon's struggles holding runners—he hadn't attempted a pickoff throw to first base since 2013, two years before signing with the Cubs in 2015—had been dissected every which way by the media and opponents.

But with left-handed hitter Jason Kipnis coming to the plate and Santana at first, Maddon believed that matchup favored Lester. So much for the "dirty inning" declaration!

With Jon replacing Kyle on the mound, I would also be coming into the game to catch, replacing Willson Contreras. That part of Joe's decision was scripted a night earlier when Maddon told me I'd come in with Jon.

Of course, the next five minutes weren't scripted. Chicago fans don't need a reminder how the fifth inning got hectic in a hurry.

◇

Jon Lester is one of the greatest pitchers—if not the greatest—I ever had the opportunity to catch. I held Jon to such a high standard, and I always expected greatness from him. You're not going to win every game, but I expected him to give his best effort every time and I wanted to give him the same. Part of what made us work so well was our personalities. I was a lot more outgoing than Jon, but I think we shared the same approach to the game. We were like brothers. You want to kick your brother's ass when he's not doing what you think he should be doing. Or what you expected.

I first met Jon in 2008, when I signed with the Boston Red Sox after I was released by the Reds. I apparently didn't make much of an impression on a guy who later became one of my closest friends. When I signed with Boston five years later, in 2013, he told me he'd almost forgotten my earlier stint with the Sox. You see, when Jon comes to work, he is there to work, not socialize. So it took me a while to get in with him. In 2013 he said I was a completely different player from what he (barely) remembered in 2008. Because I was comfortable in my role as a backup catcher, I brought tons of confidence and bravado to the clubhouse that second go-round. Jon and I quickly became great friends after that.

Jon entered the 2017 season as a four-time All-Star (2010, 2011, 2013, and 2016) and a three-time World Series champion (2007 and 2013 with the Boston Red Sox and 2016 with the Cubs). In eleven major-league seasons, his pitching record was a pretty fantastic 146-84 with a 3.44 ERA and 1,861 strikeouts. He pitched a no-hitter against the Kansas City Royals in 2008. Better yet, he is considered one of the best postseason pitchers of all time, with an ERA of 2.50.

Part of what makes him so clutch is that Jon never gets overwhelmed by the moment; he just continues to compete. Maybe that's because Jon has fought bigger battles than baseball. He, too, had fought a winning personal battle against cancer as a young man. Jon was diagnosed with anaplastic large cell lymphoma, a rare, fast-spreading, but highly treatable cancer of the lymph nodes, during his rookie season in 2006 with the Red Sox. (He was declared cancer-free in late November 2006, just before Thanksgiving.)

My craziest story about Jon comes from off the field. He helped negotiate my contract with the Cubs. Not kidding you.

◇

In early December 2014, Lester signed his six-year, $155 million contract with the Cubs. He started the 2014 season with the Red Sox but was traded to the Oakland Athletics in July for outfielder Yoenis Cespedes before becoming a free agent at the end of the sea-

son. I also was a free agent in 2014 following my second season
with the Red Sox. The Cubs, San Diego Padres, and Red Sox had
shown interest in me. The Cubs had been in communication with
my agent, Ryan Gleichowski, for several weeks and we were close
to getting a deal done. We sort of knew that they were waiting to
get Lester signed before they would really try to finish up a deal
with me. The day that Jon signed his new contract, he and a bunch
of folks, including Theo Epstein, the Cubs' president of baseball
operations, were out at a country-themed restaurant-bar called Bub
City in Chicago celebrating. It must have been two o'clock in the
morning—Hyla and I were asleep in our Tallahassee home—when
my cell phone buzzed. It was Lester. I didn't answer it because, for
one, it was two o'clock in the morning, and, two, I figured he'd call
back in the morning when I didn't answer.

Nope.

Jon called back immediately.

I was like, "What the hell?" I had watched Jon's interview earlier that day on television and figured he was out celebrating and
probably ten beers deep. Then my wife Hyla's cell phone rang, and
it was Jon's wife, Farrah. "Where's David?" she asked. It's obvious
they were out and having a great time. Jon got on the phone and
said, "Rossy, let's hammer this contract thing out. I have Theo right
here." Obviously, this was unusual, but I could tell Jon was just having fun. My wife was trying to sleep so I got up, grabbed my wife's
phone, and went into the kitchen. I thought to myself, This is hys-
terical, but I figured I would let Jon have his fun and play the conversation out. Jon asked me how much money I wanted. I was like,
"Okay, two years for $5.2 million. Now have another shot on me."

We went back and forth for fifteen minutes like that until I told
Jon I was going back to sleep.

The next morning Ryan called and I laughingly told him about the "fun negotiations" from the night before. Ryan was pissed, but he knew it was all in fun and believed that he could now pull everything together and get the deal with the Cubs finalized. He called the Cubs and busted their chops for letting Jon call me in the middle of the night. Cubs GM Jed Hoyer apologized for what happened but made it clear it was really an expression of how much they wanted me. All was good . . . Ryan just had to get it done.

By this time, it had come down to the Cubs and Padres. The Red Sox had dropped out when my contract number was higher than what they wanted to pay. San Diego called Chow the following day after Lester's late-night ring. Dave Roberts was the bench coach of the Padres at the time. He's like a big brother to me and is one of my closest friends. I learned so much from Dave when we were teammates with the Los Angeles Dodgers (2002–04). He really wanted me in San Diego. Plus, the Padres' offer continued to climb and I was like, "Oh my gosh."

The next day—day number three in this whirlwind, crazy negotiation—I left Premier Health & Fitness Center in Tallahassee. I cranked up my truck and MLB Talk was on SiriusXM Radio; it was being reported I had signed with the Padres. I checked my cell phone, which I had left in my truck, and it had a billion text messages on it. I called my agent and he had no idea where the news came from. He called the Padres and their brass said they had no idea, either. Nobody knew who had released the bogus news. I called Dave Roberts and he told me he really hoped I wouldn't sign for less money with the Cubs. The truth is I knew that it was not just about the money. Plus, I had to be a man of my word. I had told the Cubs that if we reached a certain number, then we'd hammer out the contract.

On December 23, 2014, I signed a two-year deal that included a $500,000 signing bonus and paid $2.25 million annually. The whole thing was nuts.

Thank you, Jon Lester. It's possible that if he had not called me from the bar that night, I would have ended up in San Diego and not winning the 2016 World Series.

. . . .

DAVID'S iPHONE JOURNAL
4/14/16

Boys off to a great start. We are 8–1. The atmosphere has been amazing at Wrigley. New locker room is unbelievable!!! Just swept the Reds and got Colorado coming in tomorrow. Dexter is on fire and KB is starting to heat up. Got family, parents, and sister's family in town. Nice to see everyone. Don't get to see them enough. Feel like I have eaten so much good food being back in Chicago. Every restaurant in this city has the best food.

. . . .

I started to catch Jon at the end of the 2013 season with the Red Sox and then again in 2014 before he was traded to Oakland. Over time, I understood how Jon ticked and I knew how to push his buttons to make sure he was locked in on the mound. Jon, of course, gave it back to me in heaps, too, because we both wanted to win. When we looked back on it, we laughed at some of the things we used to say to each other.

I like to have fun during games. That's my personality. When Jon and I were in Boston, Jon got four tickets behind home plate for every home game at Fenway Park. We played Detroit at home on September 3, 2013, and I asked Jon if Hyla could sit with his family for the game. He said sure. It was early in the game—maybe the second or third inning—and Jon was pitching and I was catching.

The hoopla surrounding the start of the game had calmed and I figured Hyla could hear me if I shouted at her. Before Jon started his warm-up pitches, I turned around and yelled at Hyla, "What's up girl?" and waved at her. An embarrassed Hyla put her head in her hands and gave me that "God, David, just shut up and turn around and catch" look. I also heard Jon on the mound, laughing hysterically.

Neither one of us was laughing later in the game.

Jon and Detroit's ace Max Scherzer were in a tight game. It was the top of the fifth inning and we led 1–0. With one out, Detroit catcher Brayan Pena hit a rocket that our third baseman, Will Middlebrooks, mishandled for an error. It was a tough play, but it was an error. No big deal, move on.

After Jon struck out Jose Iglesias for the second out, he surrendered consecutive ground ball singles to Austin Jackson and Torii Hunter to load the bases for Miguel Cabrera. To my eyes, Jon had made some noncompetitive pitches to Jackson and Hunter. So I strolled to the mound. I asked Jon, "Whatcha got?" Jon was pissed, but not about giving up the hits. He was still pissed about the ball Middlebrooks mishandled for an error.

I said, "You have to be fucking kidding me. You're still worried about that? That was four hitters ago." I reminded him the best hitter in the planet was up in Cabrera, and this was about to get ugly if Jon didn't get his mind right. I looked at him and said,

"Good luck with that." I turned around and walked back behind the plate.

Tough love worked that time. Jon got Cabrera to ground out to shortstop for a force at second base for the third out of the inning. We held on and won 2–1. That's one of my favorite stories, a big moment in our working relationship.

Jon and I got into one of our most memorable "discussions" in 2016 with the Cubs. It was an afternoon game at Atlanta on June 12. We had split the first two games with the Braves and were in the middle of a nine-game road trip. It was one of those southern, 95-degree sticky days where everyone hopes for a win and a quick game. Plus you always want to beat your old teams.

Like we always did, Jon and I met before the game for forty-five minutes and reviewed the scouting report on how we wanted to pitch to Atlanta hitters.

We had a plan. But then, in the bottom of the first, Jon decided to shake off my pitch selections. With one out, Chase D'Arnaud and Freddie Freeman—on a curveball Jon left up after he shook off a slider—hit consecutive singles. With Jeff Francoeur at bat, I threw wildly to third base on a double-steal attempt, and D'Arnaud scored.

I was pissed at myself for the throwing error and at Jon for not following the pitches we had just talked about in the scouting report. At the end of the inning—Atlanta led 1–0—Jon and I met in the dugout tunnel, and we went at it pretty good. I told him, "All right, I'm done. I am going to set the location where I want the pitch, and you just throw whatever you want to throw. I don't care. I'm not calling pitches anymore today. We just talked about what we wanted to throw and you're doing stupid stuff out there in the first inning. I can't deal with it."

Jon looked at me and said, "Rossy, you're going to give up on me in the first inning? It's one to nothing." I said, "Yep, I'm giving up on you." We went back and forth for another five minutes before both of us calmed down.

Jon went on to throw seven innings and allowed one run (unearned on my error) in the 13–2 victory. I maintain that error was all Jon's fault. I couldn't focus on what I was supposed to do because I was so mad at him!

◇

I didn't become Jon's personal catcher by design. It happened by chance late in the 2013 season with the Boston Red Sox. A few of his starts in a row were all against left-handed pitchers, and that was usually when I played.

We had hit it off immediately because of our personalities and desire to win. In spring training in Fort Myers, Jon, coming off his first losing season (9-14) in the big leagues, was superfocused on his mechanics. His ball was coming out flat. I remember our pitching coach, Juan, and manager, John, pointing that out in his first bull-pen I caught. I gave him some feedback on what I saw—and the coaches thought if he stayed tall, his arm angle was better. I tried to remember that and he appreciated it and respected my opinion. We just worked well together and there was an immediate mutual respect.

After I missed two months in the middle of the season with a concussion, my goal when I returned was to do anything I could to help the team win. Jarrod Saltalamacchia was the starting catcher and he helped direct the Sox's best team ERA (3.79) in thirteen years. But I started to catch Lester late in the regular season. That carried over in the American League Championship Series against the Tigers and in his two World Series victories over the St. Louis Cardinals.

Red Sox manager John Farrell liked how Lester and I performed together. From that point through the 2014 season, before Jon was traded to Oakland, Jon had a 2.77 ERA in 29 starts with me behind the plate. His ERA dipped to 1.33 in four postseason starts with me. We enjoyed the same success in Chicago. Jon won 19 games in 2016 to match his career-high, and he went 3-1 with a 2.02 ERA in six postseason games.

When Jon and I went over the scouting report before any game, I tried to be blunt, to the point, and develop a plan on how to *attack* hitters. Jon was at his best when he was aggressive and had that mindset on the mound. That aggressive approach helped solidify our bond. That's the best way I can explain it. So that's how he got stuck with me every five days.

Jon also never hid from his struggles to throw to first base with a runner on. In 2011 with Boston, he made 70 throws to first base. That number fell to 5 in 2012 and 7 in 2013. He did not attempt a single pickoff in 2014. When Jon joined the Cubs, we worked on different techniques to hold runners on at first base. We had different signs for pitchouts and modified pitchouts, like when I threw behind a runner at first base off a high, outside fastball to a right-handed hitter that wasn't intended to be a strike. Jon also altered his tempo on the mound to disrupt the baserunner. He was one of the quickest pitchers at getting the ball to me, so that gave me a chance to throw out the baserunner. I told Jon not to worry about the baserunner, let me deal with that. I wanted him to focus on the hitter and execute his pitches.

In the National League Championship Series against Los Angeles, the Dodgers' runners hopped around on the base paths and took huge leads with hopes of messing with Jon's head. He and I couldn't have cared less because most of the time, their first step or two on Jon's delivery to the plate was back to first base. I think as much as they were trying to mess with Jon, they knew I liked to back-pick.

In our 8–4 victory over Los Angeles in Game One, the tone was set when Adrian Gonzalez tried to score from second base on a single to left field. Adrian stepped back toward second base on the pitch, and he was thrown out by several steps at home plate by left fielder Ben Zobrist. Thankfully, he didn't get a good secondary lead on the pitch.

I really enjoyed trying to throw runners out and helping Jon. I had a lot of pride in my defense. In 2016, I picked off five baserunners, the most in baseball, and threw out 18 of 49 (27 percent) base stealers to match the league average.

. . . .

DAVID'S iPHONE JOURNAL
4/17/16

Room service guy tonight brought my dinner and said "tough loss today. I have my blue on. I am pulling for you guys. Don't tell my co-workers." And he pulled his pants up and showed me his Cubs socks!!! Hahaha. I learned so much baseball sitting next to Butter on the bench!!!

. . . .

While Jon and I had our last hurrah together in the 2016 World Series, Jon also pitched during my last regular-season appearance at Wrigley during his start on Sunday, September 25, against the St. Louis Cardinals. The club honored me before the game with a video tribute and gifts that, no surprise, brought me to tears. The fans gave me a standing ovation each time I came to the plate. I managed to hit a solo home run, my tenth of the season, in the fifth inning to open the scoring and received another standing ovation.

Then, with two outs in the top of the seventh and the bases empty, Joe Maddon walked to the mound to talk to Lester. I wasn't happy because Jon was in a rhythm and had pitched six scoreless innings in the 2–0 game. When I got to the mound, I asked Joe, "What the hell is going on?" He smiled and put his arm around me and said, "That's it, brother. I have never done this before but I am taking you out." It caught me off guard. The manager *never* comes to the mound to remove the catcher. It just doesn't happen.

Everyone started to tell me they loved me, and I got emotional as I realized what was going on. I pulled my mask down as tears came to my eyes and I tried to pull myself together before I walked off the field. Willson Contreras replaced me at catcher and gave me a bear hug. The entire scene was about as emotional as one can get on a pitching mound, and in such a positive way. I found out after the game that the tribute was Jon's idea. He wanted to show how much he appreciated me one last time. He approached Joe before the game and Joe felt it was the right thing to do, too, if they could pull it off.

Well, they did, and it's a moment I'll always remember.

Our journey together wasn't over, though. I caught Jon's post-season starts in Game One of the National League Division Series against San Francisco and Game One and Game Five in the National League Championship Series against Los Angeles. Jon was the winning pitcher in two of the three games.

The World Series opened in Cleveland on Tuesday, October 25. The Indians beat us 6–0 in Game One in Cleveland behind their starter, Corey Kluber. He fanned nine over six innings. Jon allowed three runs over five and two-thirds innings. The Indians struck early for a 2–0 lead in the first inning and never looked back. It was a game where the other team simply played better, end of story.

At that point, we trailed three games to one in the Series and barely sidestepped elimination in Game Five behind Jon with a 3–2 victory at Wrigley on October 30. Jon threw six innings and closer Aroldis Chapman relieved Carl Edwards Jr. for the final eight outs of the game to give the Cubs their first Series win at Wrigley Field in seventy-one years.

The game also marked my final start in the major leagues and, at that moment, possibly my last time to catch Jon. We fell behind 1–0 in the second inning but scored three in the bottom of the fourth. I capped a fourth-inning rally with a sacrifice fly to left with the bases loaded. The Indians scored a solo run off Jon in the sixth on a two-out single, and I was able to cut down Francisco Lindor at second base on an attempted steal for the final out of the inning. With two outs in the bottom of the sixth, Joe pinch-hit Miggy Montero for me. That meant Jon and I were both out of the game, since Joe intended to make a pitching change.

I never got mad at Joe too much, but I was hot about this one. I felt like I was playing well and should have remained in. Regardless, Joe made the choice and I needed to put my own feelings aside. I hugged Jon and went into the locker room to get my emotions in check. I didn't want to have a negative attitude when I returned to the dugout. I changed out of my cleats, took a few minutes to cool down, and went back out and cheered on the team.

We beat Cleveland 9–3 in Game Six to force a winner-take-all Game Seven. When Joe informed the media after Game Six that he might use Jon in relief in Game Seven, he also told me to be ready because I would catch Jon in that situation. My personal anxiety kicked in at that moment. I wanted to map out the next day, what it was going to be like, how I was going to prepare, what I needed to do to be ready. And then there was the emotional challenge of just trying to be focused and calm.

I didn't watch any film of Cleveland's hitters, but I wanted to make sure I had the scouting report on our left-handed pitcher against their hitters. I hadn't done a ton of homework on right-handed pitchers against the Indians because I always caught Jon. But when I got to Progressive Field the day of Game Seven I reviewed the report just in case I caught a right-hander out of the bullpen.

A big concern for me heading into the game was about timing—when should I walk down to the bullpen. I wanted to be in the dugout as much as possible. It was where I watched the game all year and I needed to feel the pulse of the guys. Jon pitching in relief was the big story, but you don't want it to be a distraction to the rest of the team. We decided to walk to the bullpen in the third inning, and it was crazy. Cameras appeared from every angle, and one guy somehow got in our bullpen with a camera.

My adrenaline started to pump as Jon stretched and began to warm up. He went through his entire routine and threw about thirty-five pitches. He was crisp from the start. I returned to the dugout and we scored two runs in the top of the fifth and led 4–1.

Top: Dad—with me from the beginning.

Above left: College days with Hyla after a game.

Above right: Hyla came out for my first MLB start in St. Louis.

Right: My kids running to me in the outfield after the Braves lost to the Cardinals in my first-ever wild card game in 2012. One of my favorite photos perspective-wise! I had three hits that day for the Braves, including a home run.

Above: Me and Jonny Gomes on an airboat ride in 2013 after a short day in spring training.

Below left: Night out with the boys in spring training.

Below right: On an off day with the Red Sox, Jake Peavy flew us to his place in Southern Falls, Alabama. We golfed, fished, rode four-wheelers, and bowled. It was adult Disneyland.

Ross Family Photo

ABOVE: Celebrating with family after winning the division in 2013.

BELOW: I never signed as many autographs before I became Grandpa Rossy.

Above: Before a game in September 2016. I was always keeping an eye on things.

Below left: Dressed up for a road trip, with Lack looking way smoother than me. What's in the cup, John? Joe Rule: If you wear flip-flops, toes must be painted—thanks, Landri!

Below right: Goofing around during a long rain delay in Pittsburgh.

Chicago Cubs

ABOVE: Before a road game in Atlanta with Joe and the Murray brothers.

RIGHT: I'm not the only ball player in the family! On an off day in 2016 I went home and caught one of Cole's games.

BELOW: On Friday, September 23, 2016, the Cubs honored my career before a home game. They gave me number 3 from the Wrigley score board, the plate from the day I caught Jake Arrieta's no-hitter, and my jersey from the day of my one hundredth home run.

Ross Family Photo

Chicago Cubs

ABOVE LEFT: Celebrating going to the World Series with Hyla.

ABOVE RIGHT: Cole flanked by the Lester boys—getting ready to watch their dads in Game Seven.

BELOW: My home run in Game Seven. I couldn't stop thinking about my family as I ran around the bases.

Above: The final "cock bump" with Jason Heyward.

Below: Boys carrying me off the field a champ. Doesn't get much better!

ABOVE: Taking a selfie with the boys at the Cubs Convention in January 2017. Look at that trophy!

BELOW LEFT: One of my favorite moments: in our dressing room getting psyched for our *Saturday Night Live* debut!

BELOW RIGHT: White House visit. #RetirementPlans

Ross Family Photo

Joe Maddon, pitching coach Chris Bosio, and I huddled in the dugout and Joe asked me what I thought as the bottom of the fifth approached. I told him Jon looked good, sharp in the bullpen. Joe said his goal was to go with Kyle, Lester, and Chappy (closer Aroldis Chapman) over the final four innings.

Kyle had a one-two-three, ten-pitch fourth inning—plus he had the lowest ERA in baseball at 2.13—and the thought process was to let him throw the fifth inning. Joe said, "Yeah, I'll let him go but if he gets to Kipnis, Jon is in." It was pretty important to use Jon soon if he was going to get used at all. He had started warming up a few innings earlier when Kyle was in a jam. Starters are not used to getting loosened up and then sitting back down, plus he was on short rest. I don't think Jon could have sat back down, then got loose again and been very effective. I thought using Jon there was a good idea because Kipnis had done nothing against Jon in the Series—0 for 6 with two strikeouts.

It was a really good matchup for us.

Now we just had to go out and execute it.

CHAPTER 11

A CRAZY FIVE MINUTES

10 P.M.

Cubs Lead, 5–1

Y ou've got to be kidding me."

That was the G-rated version of what I said to myself five minutes after I entered Game Seven of the World Series as a defensive replacement to catch Jon Lester out of the bullpen. Starter Kyle Hendricks was lifted having thrown just 63 pitches when he walked Carlos Santana on a 3-2 count with two outs.

With a four-run lead at 5–1 and needing one out to end the inning, we liked our chances with Lester on the mound. The left-hander—even in relief for the first time in nine years—was a good matchup for us against Cleveland's Jason Kipnis. Kipnis, the Indians' left-handed number-two hitter, had been held in check by Lester in the Series.

Lester had a 2-2 count on Kipnis when he hit a dribbler in front of the plate. I fielded the ball, turned to first, and let it rip.

Shit.

139

The ball sailed to the side of Anthony Rizzo, well out of his reach at first base for an error. Santana raced to third and Kipnis advanced to second. I was upset with myself because I didn't have a good grip on the ball, rushed the throw, and almost got Rizzo killed as it went down the right-field line in foul territory.

Still, despite my throwing error, we still had two outs with the chance to close out a clean inning on the scoreboard.

Right-handed-hitting Francisco Lindor, who was 4-for-9 with three strikeouts in his career against Lester, was up next. After a first-pitch strike, Jon spiked a curveball in front of the plate that bounced off the dirt and struck the front of my mask. The ball ricocheted to my right toward our dugout on the first base line and the on-deck circle.

Everything happened in a split second. I stumbled to my left, away from the ball, and used my glove hand to brace my fall. I took off my mask with my right hand in the same motion. By the time I got to the ball near our dugout—sliding to pick it up and throwing back to Lester covering the plate—both runs had scored on the wild pitch. Kipnis never hesitated on the play from second base, and he made a nice slide under Jon's sweeping tag.

It was one of those moments where the game sped up on me. I was in for only a few minutes and . . . how the hell had these two plays happened? Suddenly I did feel like a grandpa—the old man who tripped over his own two feet. I was supposed to be the guy who prevented runs. They didn't put me in for my offense.

I was pissed with myself, but I got my emotions in check and reminded myself we still had the lead. Now our job was limiting the damage.

Lester struck out Lindor on a 3-2 count to end the inning. But the Indians sliced our margin to 5–3 and had new life.

I found out later how bad the wild pitch looked when that ball, after it bounced in front of the plate, hit off my mask and I went back down. It looked as if I had gotten my bell rung. I couldn't figure out why reporters kept asking me after the game if I was all right. Of course I'm all right, we just won the World Series. Little did everyone know I just tripped over my own two feet. Due to my history with concussions, they were just concerned for me. When I finally got to watch it, I saw what they were talking about.

This time it wasn't about my noggin, though.

· · · · · · · · · · · · · · ·

DAVID'S iPHONE JOURNAL
5/11/16

"Hopefully we can look up at the end of the year and have earned what people said about us."

—Theo Epstein

· · · · · · · · · · · · · · ·

I suffered multiple concussions during my fifteen-year career in the major leagues, most coming from repeated foul tips off my face mask. But what's even more startling was how uneducated I was about concussions, including symptoms, detection, and the long-term effects. There are different types of concussions, and the medical field is still learning about the dangers of a single concussion and the multiplier of repeated concussions.

When you think of baseball, you probably don't think of concussions. Baseball is considered a noncontact sport, especially when you compare it to football, hockey, boxing, basketball, and wrestling. Still, there are collisions and injuries in baseball and most times they are unavoidable. Let's not also forget that many pitchers are throwing 100 mph these days, and a helmet will provide a hitter only so much protection. What makes concussions scary, no matter the sport, is that they can't be seen on Xrays and attempts to prevent them have been difficult. Concussions, I've heard, are the most difficult injuries physicians have to treat. Of course, it doesn't help that so many of us athletes feel like we can push through anything. I've learned that's not the case, even when you're conflicted emotionally because you don't want to let down your teammates.

One of the most violent collisions I was involved in occurred in August 2007, when I was with the Cincinnati Reds. San Diego's Mike Cameron leveled me when he scored from second base on a single by Khalil Greene in the top of the third inning.

At the plate, Cameron, at six foot two and 210 pounds, flattened me and knocked the ball out of my glove. My head gear flew off and the back of my head hit the ground. I was knocked unconscious momentarily, and, quite honestly, I still can't really remember that day. But, after the collision, I didn't want to come out of the game no matter how I felt.

Our starting pitcher, Bronson Arroyo, struck out Rob Mackowiak for the third out. A few minutes later, I led off the bottom of the third inning with an infield single to first base off Jake Peavy. When I got to first base, our first base coach, Billy Hatcher, said "That a baby." I replied, "Yeah, I'll take a one-for-two with a walk." The thing was, I had only been to the plate once that day. Hatch asked for time and called the trainers to come get me. The Reds trainers saw I was off-kilter and confused and Javier Valentin entered as a pinch runner and replaced me at catcher.

In the dugout, I repeatedly asked my teammates when I was scheduled to bat. I didn't remember my at-bat from a few minutes earlier. I also went back and forth into the video room to watch a replay of the collision at home plate, not remembering I had watched it only moments earlier. When the team physician asked me what year it was, I said 2003 as a joke. But then I said, "No, no, just kidding, it is 2005," and it wasn't a joke anymore. I was sent to the hospital for testing. My wife, Hyla, and our infant daughter, Landri, did not attend the game but they met me there.

At the hospital, I recognized Hyla and Landri, but I couldn't recall my daughter's birth when asked. Later that night at our home, I repeatedly asked Hyla a series of questions. Ouch, my head hurts, what happened? She would tell me, then I would say, "Was the runner out?" "Did I hold on to the ball?" "Did we win?" She told me I asked those questions every five minutes and listened to her response as if I had never heard it explained.

When Hyla asked me, "Don't you remember, I just told you?" I got irritated and agitated. It reached the point where Hyla had to walk outside to talk to the Reds' trainer, family, and friends when they called to check on me. I know Hyla was scared, because I repeatedly told her I felt okay.

And she knew I wasn't.

◇

During the 2016 baseball season, I was one of eight players in Major League Baseball who went on the disabled list with a concussion. I missed five games and eight days before the July All-Star break after taking a foul ball off my face mask against the Cincinnati Reds. I also was placed on the seven-day disabled list in July 2015 during my first season in Chicago with a mild concussion after I took a couple of foul balls off the face mask against the New York Mets. I joked to sportswriters that I felt "a little off" for a couple of days, but "I'm probably always a little off. It's hard to tell what's normal for me."

I explained the feeling to Hyla as one of fogginess. That feeling might be accompanied by a headache, but I just felt foggy, sluggish, tired. Hyla's explanation was more heartfelt. She said I was "there, but not there" when she looked into my eyes. Again, as an athlete, there's no visible signs of a concussion, so to the viewing public everything must be okay. I didn't have a cast, and I didn't need surgery. I could still throw a ball and swing a bat. I had my bell rung and I just needed to shake it off. No big deal. Right?

Nothing could be further from the truth.

I learned the seriousness of concussions during the 2013 season with the Red Sox. I lost more than two months to the most severe series of concussions in my career. It was a scary, dark time and I honestly thought my career might be over.

It was Saturday, May 11, 2013. We were playing Toronto at Fenway. I started at catcher and played nearly the entire game before being removed for a pinch hitter in the bottom of the ninth inning. I had taken several foul balls off my face mask during the game, including back-to-back foul tips near my forehead that sent paint chips flying off my mask.

Greg Gibson was the umpire that day and he asked me several times if I was all right. He told me he was behind the plate when Mike Matheney got his career-ending concussion and that it was nothing to mess with. Turns out Gibson had had his fair share, too.

Hyla watched the game from the children's playroom at Fenway Park, where she held a party for our son Cole's fourth birthday. On the walk to our apartment near Fenway Park following the game,

Hyla sensed I wasn't engaged in the conversation. She showed me photographs from the party, but I really wasn't interested. She asked me if I was okay and, of course, I said I was fine.

When we got to the apartment, Hyla still was concerned—especially when I started to cry for no reason as I looked at Cole's birthday photos. Hyla had seen enough. She didn't have the telephone numbers to Boston's training staff in her telephone, so, unbeknownst to me, she headed up two floors to teammate Dustin Pedroia's apartment. Dustin, a type A personality, followed Hyla down to our apartment to make sure I was okay. They came in the front and in true Peddy fashion, Dustin asked, "Hey, bro, your eggs scrambled?" I told both of them I was fine, but mind over matter doesn't always work. The Red Sox placed me on the seven-day concussion disabled list the following day.

I returned to the team May 25 but I stunk for a good two to three weeks. Now, I'm used to having rough patches but this was even brutal for me. I struck out five times (four times swinging) in my first game back on the twenty-fifth, against the Indians. I've been known to strike out, but five times in one game? I went 3-for-22 but continued to play because I thought I was okay and getting better. I simply thought my timing was off at the plate.

But it was strange. I saw the ball out of the pitcher's hand, but it kind of disappeared when I swung. I tried to make a few adjustments at the plate, but nothing worked. I watched film of one game where I went to throw a guy out at second base and instead heaved the ball clear into right field. I would slam two Red Bull energy drinks and a 5-hour Energy drink so I could bring my normal energy to the park every day. I felt energy was my responsibility as a catcher and I needed to do whatever was necessary to bring it. But I could never get to the level I needed. It also seemed like I had a headache every day, but I kept saying I wasn't worried. I thought I'd wake up the next morning and it would be gone.

I continued to grind away and even took another foul tip off the face mask against Baltimore on June 14. I never told anyone, but the next day during batting practice in Baltimore, I threw up in between rounds. I would later learn that all of these episodes displayed classic concussion symptoms.

Hyla remained concerned because she saw a noticeable difference in me off the field. I was short with the kids, and they'd cry because of the way I looked at them. Hyla covered for me and told the kids I had a headache. Things came to a head one evening when we went out to dinner in Boston. We got to the restaurant but I didn't eat much, complaining of all the noise and commotion around me. Then, during our drive back to our apartment, a guy cut me off in traffic. I completely lost it, and screamed at the guy at the top of my lungs. When we stopped at the red light, I was ready to get out of my car and beat the shit out of him. But Hyla grabbed my shirt and wouldn't let go. The kids were crying and it was a bad scene.

Upset, Hyla told me she planned to reach out to the team's medical director, Dr. Larry Ronan, if I didn't do so first. So before our home game against Tampa Bay on June 18, I talked to Larry. Of course, I told Larry I felt fine and was only following Hyla's request. But Larry didn't believe me, and he telephoned Hyla. Hyla told Larry everything that had happened, and she felt so bad because she thought she threw me under the bus. I was emotional because I didn't want my teammates to think I was bowing out on them and letting everyone down. I wasn't swinging the bat well and if my teammates thought I just didn't want to be out there because I wasn't playing well, that would have killed me. I knew

how uneducated I was about concussions and figured most players were the same.

The Red Sox pulled me off the bench prior to our game and
placed me back on the DL.

◇

On June 18, the Red Sox contacted Dr. Micky Collins, a concussion
specialist at UPMC/University of Pittsburgh Schools of Health Sci-
ences in Pittsburgh.

I should have known I'd hit it off with Micky. He's a huge Boston Red Sox fan and was a former baseball player, too. He played
for the University of Southern Maine in the 1989 Division III College World Series.

The trip to Pittsburgh was the first step in my road to recovery.

When I first met Micky, however, I still tried to put a positive
spin on my health. I wanted to do anything I could not to be sick.
I wanted to get back to Boston and my teammates. My plan didn't
work. Micky quickly realized once he started to ask me questions
that I had multiple issues. He's good at what he does. About fifteen minutes into his evaluation, Micky could see I was not doing
well. I was light sensitive, tired, and had headaches. I even vomited
during the testing. It was obvious my brain wasn't working the way
it should.

Micky wanted me to think about the brain as an egg yolk inside
an eggshell. And no matter what kind of helmet a player is wear-
ing around his head, even if it's great protective equipment when it
comes to catching, if you get a foul tip hard enough, the egg yolk
will move inside the shell. It's an injury that needs time and rest to
heal properly.

He said there are six types of concussions, identified by the symptoms they exhibit: vestibular (balance issues), ocular (vision problems), mood, anxiety, migraine headaches, and cervical (problems with the neck). He said most concussion sufferers exhibit several of these symptoms, but one or two symptoms tend to predominate. Unfortunately, I hit the concussion lotto. He didn't tell me this until I was better. He just kept stressing the plan for recovery and that my career wasn't going to be over. Micky said I showed symptoms of all six. When you think of those six different types of concussions as interlocking circles, he explained how this injury can affect a person in a pretty robust way.

Micky explained the vestibular system is one people take for granted. It's a system that allows us to interpret movement and motion, to balance, and to stabilize our vision when we move our head. It allows us to exercise and not feel anything. And when the system is decompensated from the injury, patients have a sense of fogginess.

Micky said 60 to 70 percent of our brain is devoted to our ocular movements—vision. This kind of concussion can lead to problems with focusing on your vision and eye movement. That's not good when a player is in the batter's box trying to hit a 95 mph heater or a spinning curveball. The remaining concussions listed above are self-explanatory but none of them are good.

Micky promised me three things during that initial visit. As an athlete who was accustomed to following a plan, I was encouraged. He promised me that he'd get me better and back on the field if I did everything they asked of me—and did it correctly. Despite the number of issues I experienced, he said each of them was treatable. He promised he wouldn't put me back on the field until I was healthy and it was safe to do so. And he promised he wouldn't hold me out a day longer than I needed to be held out because he understood how important it was for me to return to my team.

Collins and his clinicians have devised a number of tests, including one called VOMS (vestibular ocular motor screening), to diagnose and treat concussions. I had to place my thumb in front of my eyes and track it with my eyes as I moved it back and forth. I underwent a series of balance and movement tests, stuff I should have been able to do in my sleep. Stuff I took for granted when I played, like starting in a catcher's crouch and moving laterally while looking side to side and up and down. I still used these tests when I got a good foul ball to the mask to make sure I was symptom-free. The first time I tried it with Micky, I became so nauseated that I threw up.

After my seven-hour visit with Micky and his team that first day, I was so drained that I could barely lift my head when Hyla and I got to Pittsburgh International Airport for our flight home.

Once my diagnosis was clear and I understood that the symptoms were treatable, I felt a huge sense of relief. I know there was concern I might not return to the team in 2013, but Micky felt confident I would.

But healing would take months, and not weeks.

· · · · · · · · · · · · · · · ·

DAVID'S iPHONE JOURNAL
5/13/16

It's been awhile! Haha. So much has gone on!! The first month has been amazing, we are rolling. We are 19-6, having fun, kicking everyone's ass. I got to catch Jake's no-hitter, that was a blast. I am off to a decent start. Got two homers!! Got two nights with O'Flaherty when Braves were in town. Had a rainout so had some good hang time. Went to dinner at Chicago Cut. Miggy got hurt so I have been playing a little more. Fed is up, he had a great game tonight. If my body holds up I think I'll have a good year. I am enjoying playing. Kind of a long stretch away from family. They are coming in this weekend at home. I can't wait to hang with them. They are so busy at home. I think Hyla could use a break, too. Can't wait until they are here all summer. Really want to play with my kids.

• • • • • • • • • • • • • • • •

Micky decided it was best for my recovery if I returned home to Tallahassee rather than rejoin the team in Boston. He wanted me away from that environment to focus on my rehab.

I underwent a three-part therapy regimen. Micky treated my vestibular problems with vestibular therapy. It's not by rest, but by exposure and stressing the system. A second therapy was vision therapy. I had to retrain my eyes to work together again. And the third included certain movements that would help recalibrate both the vestibular and ocular systems. I also was prescribed medication to help in my recovery.

By the All-Star break in July, I actually felt a lot better—so good, in fact, that Hyla, the kids, and I went to Orange Beach in the Florida Panhandle to meet Tim Hudson, my former teammate at Auburn and with the Braves, and his family for a day of boating and tubing.

Hyla didn't think the trip was a good idea—and, of course, she was right. It was like I went on a daylong bender that didn't include booze, but I still ended up queasy and sick. That day of fun set me back in my recovery a few weeks, but by late July I was feeling healthy—and restless.

I needed to get back to Boston with my teammates. Micky agreed and the plan was to slowly reexpose me to that environment and baseball-related activities. Even that was a process. I could watch three innings, then I had to go home; four innings the next day and so on. I visited Micky's office three more times, and that doesn't include the hours Hyla and I talked to him on the telephone.

Finally, on August 18, 2013, I was cleared to rejoin the Red Sox. We know how that magic carpet ride ended—with a World Series championship over the St. Louis Cardinals behind a 6–1 victory in Game Six. I caught the final out in the ninth inning, Three months earlier, I couldn't play with my children without getting dizzy.

I owe a ton of thanks to the Red Sox, Dr. Ronan, and especially Dr. Micky Collins. I don't know what path my life would have taken if not for him. He saved my career and helped me to become a two-time World Series champ. Thanks, Mick!

◇

In March 2011, Major League Baseball and the Major League Baseball Players Association adopted a new series of protocols under the new joint policy regarding concussions, including the creation of a seven-day disabled list.

The story on MLB.com detailed how "a committee of experts created the policy, which will oversee the manner in which concussions are diagnosed initially and will be used to determine when players and umpires can return to the field following a concussion." The new policy went into effect on opening day that year. The biggest change the policy brought was the creation of a seven-day disabled list for concussions, which was aimed to allow suitable time for concussions to clear and prevent players from returning too early, according to the story. All four major professional sports leagues in the United States and Canada now have concussion policies.

The MLB concussion policy is a good thing. However, I would probably urge the league to continue tweaking the policy as the research is evolving.

I would urge every player to see a specialist, even if the incident in question felt minor. For me, the most dangerous thing was the second and third blows to the head. Seeing someone who deals in this field daily will also allow the player to become more educated and more self-aware.

When I first came back in 2013 after my time on the DL, they put me through a pretty tough, physical routine, which I got through easily. But that was because my issue was vestibular, and not really heart-rate stuff. The more I moved my head and the busier the environment was, the crazier things got for me. My eyes couldn't really process things rapidly. I definitely think MLB can be a little better when it comes to testing all the different ways that a concussion can affect you. Right now they do some physical activities and memory testing and ask a lot of questions. But the test is vague about what a good response is. Is testing where it needs to be? Probably not yet, but I think MLB is moving in the right direction.

The seriousness of concussions hit home for me when Ryan Freel, a friend and a teammate from my time with the Reds, died of a self-inflicted gunshot wound on December 22, 2012, in Jacksonville, Florida. He was thirty-six. Ryan's career in the major leagues was cut short after eight years due to head and other injuries.

Ryan and I had played together on a Junior Olympic team as teenagers. Ryan also attended Tallahassee Community College, so we had lots of mutual friends. In Cincinnati, we even lived next door to each other. He was one of those exciting players who play at 100 mph and do anything needed to win. He showed no fear on the field and gave up his body to make an out or otherwise help his team.

Nearly a year after his death, Freel was the first MLB player to be diagnosed with chronic traumatic encephalopathy (CTE), according to researchers at the Boston University School of Medicine. CTE is a progressive degenerative disease found in people who have had a severe blow or repeated blows to the head.

Ryan's death really hit me hard. As a player, sometimes you wonder what you are doing it for. You play the game because you love it. And when it's over and it's time to retire, you head home to enjoy the memories, kick back, and relax. But you do worry about what you put your body through, and I constantly think about it.

Sometimes if I fly off the handle at the kids, I wonder where that anger or snap comes from. The short temper I think we all have, but is that normal or is it not normal? Where's my excuse? Can I blame it on having concussions, or do I simply need to learn to have more patience?

I am constantly fighting those battles in my head, trying to figure out where my reaction is coming from. I still get a little annoyed with traveling and busy environments, like airports. Loud, crowded spaces—they are tough for me to deal with.

Baseball has been good to me, except in this one area.

CHAPTER 12

SMALL REDEMPTION

10:07 P.M.

Cubs Lead, 5–3

A wild throw, a leg-tangling wild pitch, and, just like that, I had allowed two runs to score in the bottom of the fifth inning of Game Seven of the World Series. There are times in games, especially in the playoffs, when every pitch, every play, and every at-bat counts, and this was one of the moments. Players are under intense pressure, but that's no excuse for making errors.

As upset as I was, I didn't have much time to dwell on those five crazy minutes. I was scheduled to bat second in the top of the sixth inning, and I needed to calm down and get my thoughts in order.

After Lester struck out Lindor to end the fifth inning, I looked his way as we walked back to the dugout, mouthing, "Sorry, buddy." He gave me that "Don't worry about it" look. He is such a pro!

As far as the other guys, everything said to me back in the dugout was positive and quick. Everyone was focused on the top of the sixth inning. We still had a two-run lead, 5–3.

Trying to shove aside my disappointment in my play, I took off my catcher's gear, grabbed my batting helmet and bat, and headed to the on-deck circle.

Andrew Miller had come in to relieve Cleveland starter Corey Kluber. Andrew, a six-foot-seven left-hander and a former teammate of mine in Boston, is one of the best relievers in the game. I caught him a bunch of times in Boston, so I knew what to expect.

Miller's slider is nasty. It's a pitch I don't think I could hit even if I knew it was coming. It's that filthy. A former first-round selection out of the University of North Carolina in 2006, Andrew started his Major League Baseball career primarily as a starting pitcher. He moved to full-time relief in 2012, and served in all three roles—middle relief, setup, and closing.

The odds against Miller were not in our favor—or mine. Heading into the 2016 World Series, the Indians had won the last 16 games in which Miller had pitched. I faced Andrew in Cleveland's 6–0 win in Game One of the Series in Cleveland, and it didn't end well for me. I struck out swinging on an 84 mph slider out of the strike zone on a 3-2 count with the bases loaded.

Cubs shortstop Addison Russell led off the top of the sixth, and Miller got him to pop out to Cleveland first baseman Mike Napoli in foul territory for the first out.

My turn.

My intention was to take Miller's first pitch, no matter where it came. In the back of my mind, though, I knew he might throw me a first-pitch fastball. Second-guessing myself, I swung through a first-pitch slider inside.

My emotions still were running high. I told myself to relax and wait until I saw a pitch I could hit. Miller's next pitch was another slider—this time right down the middle. I didn't swing. Strike two.

Earlier in the season, I had changed my approach at the plate when I faced a count with two strikes. I choked up on the bat for better control and squatted a tad in my stance to shorten my stride. I also moved slightly closer to the plate to take away the outside strike. Prior to the 2016 season, I never had a two-strike approach at all. After Joe Maddon talked about the importance of a two-strike strategy in spring training, it really changed my year. I hit six or seven of my ten home runs during the regular season with two strikes.

With an 0-2 count, I just wanted to battle. I had no intention of making it an easy at-bat for Miller.

Miller threw me a fastball, up and away. Ball one. The thing was, I saw that fastball really well. I told myself that if he threw that one again, I would see it. When Miller was set on the mound and looked in for his sign from catcher Roberto Perez, he shook off the next pitch.

I had watched video of Miller and noticed he shook to a fastball a lot. He liked to throw his slider—and threw it about 60 percent of the time, according to our scouting reports—so when he shook, it usually meant a fastball would be coming.

For whatever reason, this time I expected a heater. If he had thrown a slider, I probably would have swung and missed. But instead he hurled a fastball right down in the zone where I like it. I put a great swing on it and felt my bat make solid contact.

I knew I hit it pretty well, but it was to straightway center field—the hardest part of the ball park to hit a home in. Did it have enough to carry over?

I saw Indians center fielder Rajai Davis running back and I actually remember thinking, Aw, man, do not rob me of this home run. I was going to run right out of the tunnel and go home if he caught it. When I saw Davis jump and the ball sail over his glove and out of the park—it traveled an estimated 358 feet—I was just so thankful.

The first thought that crossed my mind as I rounded first base was, Well, at least I got a run back for us. I had given up two and, boom, I got one back. It was now 6–3.

Later I found out that, at 39 years, 228 days, I was the oldest player to hit a home run in Game Seven of a World Series. The previous record was held by the Pirates' Willie Stargell, who was 39 years, 225 days old when he socked one in Game Seven of the 1979 World Series. It also was my second home run of the 2016 postseason. I hit a home run in the National League Division Series against the Giants to become the oldest catcher to hit a home in postseason history, surpassing the Angels' Bob Boone from the 1986 American League Championship Series and the Indians' own Tony Pena from the 1995 American League Division Series. Records are nice—we old guys have to stick together—but the record books were the furthest thing from my mind as I rounded the bases in Game Seven.

I also found out later that my wife, Hyla, had called my home run from the stands—with help from "Memaw." It had been a long and trying day for Hyla as she dealt with our son, Cole, who was feeling ill. He was still feeling miserable and Hyla just wanted to go somewhere and put her son to bed. She actually nearly missed the team bus to the field from the hotel on account of Cole. Since we had checked out of the Westin, Hyla thought she'd have to make a reservation at a different hotel and possibly miss the game. In the end, they all made it to the stadium—Hyla, Cole, and my daughter Landri.

I didn't help Hyla's stress level in the fifth inning when I allowed those two runs to score on my wild throw and tangled feet. Hyla was next to my agent, Ryan Gleichowski, in the stands. After that mess of an inning, Ryan hurried off and purchased two vodka drinks—a double for Hyla and a single for him. When Hyla asked why he didn't buy himself a double, Ryan said, "Oh no, I saw them make yours."

When I came to bat in the sixth, Cole was seated next to Hyla, and Landri was behind Hyla in the next row. When Cole stood on his seat so he could see, Hyla leaned over and asked Cole during my at-bat if he thought his Memaw was watching.

"Memaw" was my grandmother who had lived outside of Tallahassee in Havana and watched or listened to all of my games until she died in 2015. Cole said he didn't know, but Hyla told Cole she thought Memaw was watching. And that maybe "she could help carry Dad's ball over the fence." Just after Hyla said that to Cole, I hit the solo home run. Hyla said it was such a surreal and emotional moment for her in the stands, the first time she had ever asked for help from a "guardian angel."

I was all business during my home run trot around the bases. I remember first base coach Brandon Hyde yelled when the ball sailed over the fence as I rounded the bag. Third base coach Gary Jones smiled slightly but still looked serious when he reached out to shake my hand as I rounded third base. This wasn't on my mind, but before the season began, I had made a bet with Kyle Schwarber and our traveling secretary, Vijay Tekchandani, that if I hit 10 home runs in 2016, I'd postpone my retirement. I actually finished with 12 home runs (10 in the regular season and 2 in the postseason) but I knew the timing was right. And little did I realize my story would end in such dramatic fashion.

I clapped a few times as I neared home plate, but I intentionally didn't show much emotion rounding the bases. I was in full concentration mode. The moment wasn't about me hitting a home run as much as it was getting a run back for us. We also had four more innings of work left—*don't get too excited, we ain't done nothing yet.* Anything can happen at any time. That's why sports are exciting.

Plus, with all the adrenaline surrounding the Series and the season, I was such an emotional wreck inside anyway. By the end of the postseason, your body and mind are just worn out. It was as if the World Series were a season in itself. The start of the playoffs seemed like months ago—another time, another universe.

I thought if I released any emotion as I rounded the bases, I might totally exhaust my supply. I was running on fumes. Remember, I am a grandpa!

Finally, as I reached home plate, I let a little bit out. My only thought was of my family. I wanted to give my Hyla, Landri, and Cole a little love. I raised both arms and pointed their way in the stands behind home plate.

As I headed to the dugout, the first player waiting for me was, of all people, right fielder Jason Heyward. Uh oh. He was giving me a look that could only mean one thing: the "cock bump." It's nuts, right? I am thinking, It is Game Seven of the World Series, let's get back to work, and Jason wants to do the cock bump?

The name doesn't leave much to the imagination. Jason leaned to his left and raised his right leg, and I leaned to my left and raised my right leg, and we celebrated my home run by banging our protective cups against each other. Then Dexter Flower appeared next to me. Boom, another cock bump. So now I think, Screw it, I've got to cock-bump everyone in this dugout.

I had to laugh when I thought about it after the game. I suppose it was karma that Jason Heyward was the first player to greet me after I hit the home run. I came up with the idea of the cock bump when I played with the Braves from 2009 to 2012. The story is kind of funny, if a little crude, and I'll explain it after I tell you what an incredible man Jason Heyward is.

I met Jason, a top prospect for the Braves, when we played in Atlanta together. Fast-forward to December 2015. After Jason signed his eight-year, $184 million contract with the Cubs, one of the first things he did was to tell the team he wanted to pay for a hotel suite for me and my family on the team's road trips during the 2016 season. It would cost a whopping $30,000. Jason said I served as a mentor to him during our three years together in Atlanta—we were locker mates when Jason made his major-league debut in 2010—and the hotel suite was his way of thanking me.

On January 13—two days before the Cubs' thirty-first annual winter fan convention at the Sheraton Grand Chicago—the team's traveling secretary, Vijay Tekchandani, informed me of Jason's gesture. It enabled me to comfortably spend time with my family on the road. I could barely believe it.

I immediately fired off a text message to Jason: "Bro, Vijay just informed me you are hooking me up on the road!! You don't have to do that buddy!!! . . . But if it puts me closer to your room then I'm in! Ha! Thank you buddy!! Don't get freaked out when I give you a giant hug tomorrow!!! Love you brother." Jason replied: "I welcome it Rossy! Thanks for being a part of what got me to where I am today! Love you too! *U Welcome."

Jason's amazing gift was such a cool and emotional start to my final season.

· · · · · · · · · · · · · · · ·

DAVID'S iPHONE JOURNAL
5/15/16

It's funny to think about what you hear from fans. "Hit your 100th homer today" or "call a no-hitter today." Hahaha, I love it!!! Our fans are coming to the games to see something special. That should tell you a lot about our team! And, the boys try to do it every game. Lester took a no-hitter into the seventh inning today. He had some nasty stuff today. The Pittsburgh team is a tough lineup. On my way to the airport. Lester is letting me use his plane hours again. This dude has done this like five times for me to be with my family. Get to take them to school, which is the best, and Cole has a baseball game. Maybe some pool time!

· · · · · · · · · · · · · · ·

After I left the Dodgers in 2004, I bounced around the league. Over the next four years, I played for the Pirates, the Padres, and the Reds. I spent the last part of the 2008 season with the Red Sox but became a free agent at the end of the year. I was the definition of a baseball journeyman, so when I signed a two-year contract with the Braves on December 5, 2008, I was thrilled to have the stability of a perennially successful club.

I met Jason Heyward for the first time during spring training in 2009 at the Braves' complex in Orlando, Florida. An athletic outfielder, Jason was a first-round selection in the 2007 Major League Amateur Draft out of Henry County High School in McDonough, Georgia, thirty-two miles outside Atlanta. Jason started his minor-league career at age seventeen and was considered one of the organization's top prospects.

During spring training that year I shook Jason's hand and said, "Good to meet you," but I didn't spend much time with him, simply because we were headed in opposite directions. He was sent to the minor leagues and I had to focus on my first season with the club. Jason flourished in the minors, with both *Baseball America* and *USA Today* naming him their Minor League Player of the Year. In 2010, everyone knew Jason had a chance to make the big-league team out of spring training. The guy hit bombs all over the place. One of his tape-measure home runs during batting practice at the Champion Stadium training complex in Lake Buena Vista, Florida, dented a Coca-Cola truck in the parking lot.

Jason had started most of our spring training games and was doing all the right things—getting to games early, getting his at-bats, getting his work in, and getting his rest. He made a good impression on everyone and didn't do anything stupid. But, as a rookie, there was always a teachable moment around the corner.

We had a road game during spring training in Port St. Lucie, against the Mets. The starters were broken down into three groups, and those groups hit first. When you weren't hitting, you were in the outfield shagging balls. And once those three groups are done, those players can head into the locker room while the remaining players on the trip bat. Jason wasn't in the starting lineup that game, but he still was scheduled to hit with the first three groups.

When he was finished shagging and hitting, he went into the locker room like he had always done. I followed him into the locker and shouted, "J-Hey!" I had a serious tone, but I also had a smile inside because I didn't want to bust out laughing—even if I needed to air him out in front of the team to make a point. Jason answered, "What's up, Rossy?"

I asked Jason if he was in the starting lineup today, and he said no. I said, "Okay, if you're not starting I need you to get your ass outside for the rest of the BP group and shag with the rest of us nonstarters. That's the way it goes. If you're playing, you don't shag the whole time. If you're not playing, you shag the whole BP and then come inside."

Jason wore it well and said, "Okay, my bad, Rossy, it won't happen again." About that time, pitcher Billy Wagner, a sixteen-year veteran who played his final season in the majors that year in Atlanta, saw Jason and laughed. "God dang, kid," he said, "you are already messing up."

That was how I welcomed Jason to the big leagues.

Jason's locker was next to mine in Atlanta for three years. It was obvious the guy was a special talent and a special person. Heck, in his major-league debut against the Chicago Cubs on April 5, 2010, he hit a home run on the first pitch he saw. Jason finished his first major-league season with a .277 batting average with 18 home runs. He also reached base in 36 consecutive games and made the All-Star team.

But numbers and honors are only part of the game. There are tons of guys who are great talents but aren't great teammates. I wanted Jason to know that I cared for him as a person and as a player. He was a guy who listened first and talked second, if at all; he wanted to do the right things. Jason respected the game and respected his teammates. He was that way in Atlanta and in Chicago when we were teammates. Jason's struggles in 2016 were dissected by the media but he was a huge part of our success. We were World Series champions because of what Jason did for our team, including the players-only meeting he called during the rain delay of Game Seven. You take a piece out of that winning formula, who knows what happens. Everyone has a good year when you are World Series champions!

I always wanted to be the guy my teammates depended on, the guy who was consistent in my approach. I demanded the best out of myself and the best out of my teammates. The constant thought in my head was, Why are we all here? Let's try to make each other better and try to win as many games as possible. That was part of the message I wanted to convey to my teammates, including Jason.

And Jason Heyward soaked it all in, becoming one of the great teammates I've ever had.

. . . .

DAVID'S iPHONE JOURNAL
5/17/16

Home was amazing! Got to pitch to Cole's Atom League team. That was cool. Cole said, "Dad, I was trying to impress you." Funny what goes on in those little brains. He doesn't even know he impresses me every day. We got beat tonight, got to get a win tomorrow!! Starting a long road trip, need to get off to a good start. When you win so much, you lose one or two games, losing feels terrible!! "We'll see."

. . . .

After Jason played five seasons with the Braves and one season with the Cardinals in 2015 (the Cubs beat the Cardinals three games to one in the National League Division Series that year) he became a free agent for the first time. One of the first things he did after he signed with us was pay for hotel suites for myself and assistant hitting coach Eric Hinske on our road trips. The suites made a huge difference in terms of comfort for my family.

Eric also was a teammate of Jason in Atlanta before he retired in 2013, following twelve seasons in the big leagues. Atlanta was a special place and time for all of us. The three of us had a unique bond from our days there. Jason was a teenager when he started professionally and now he was a grown-ass man. Jason wanted to show his appreciation and thank me and Eric for everything we shared and worked so hard for in Atlanta. He didn't pay for our suites for any recognition. He was just thoughtful and generous, and he wanted me to be able to spend quality time with my family on the road and be comfortable. A suite was a luxury that I wasn't accustomed to. The extra space was perfect for when the kids played, especially our youngest, Harper. She was able to run around from room to room. Plus, when she needed to go down for a nap, she had a room of her own. Jason's gesture helped make the road trips, and my last season, a whole new set of memories for me and the family.

When we played in Miami against the Marlins, our team hotel—and my suite at the St. Regis Bal Harbour Resort—was on Miami Beach. It was a two-bedroom suite and the balcony felt like it was a hundred yards long. It has a great pool for the kids and we spent a lot of time on the beach, too. My parents made the drive from Tallahassee to Miami, so that made it even more fun. The family also joined me for a cool trip to San Francisco. We went to the redwood forest and hiked. It was a lot of fun to get up early and spend time with my family.

Jason's struggles in 2016 were well documented. He batted .230 with a career-low seven home runs and was replaced in the lineup in the postseason. It was a difficult season for him, but he never complained. I saw Jason at his best, and I saw him have a tough year. But I know his behavior, his mindset, his mentality. He's a stand-up guy who will never make an excuse. Baseball is a humbling game and it will humble every player at some point. It's a game of failure and the key is how you handle that adversity. It will bury you if you're not careful. Jason was there for me in 2016 100 percent of the time, and I will always be there for him 100 percent of the time. I'm glad I got to spend my last season in the big leagues with Jason. I was there when his big-league career started in Atlanta, and he was with me when mine ended in Chicago. That was pretty cool.

◇

Did you think I was going to forget to tell you the origin story of the "cock bump"? Fear not.

One day when I was playing for the Braves I found myself sitting in a hotel room watching a story on ESPN about how Dusty Baker invented the high-five in 1977, when he slapped the hand of Glenn Burke after Dusty hit his thirtieth home run on the final day of the season. I thought to myself, The high-five is taken, so what can I invent?

I wanted to invent a shared gesture between two players to celebrate when one of them hit a home run. Suddenly an image flashed through my head—a painless, if slightly questionable, maneuver. Of all the physical gestures the human body is capable of making, why not the "cock bump"? Well, why not?

Basically, players bumped their protective cups together to celebrate a home run.

While we celebrated home runs that way while I was with Atlanta, I had actually forgotten about the cock bump until Heyward reminded me of it when he signed with the Cubs. He said, "Dude, where is the cock bump? We need to bring back the cock bump." I said, "Hell yeah, I am bringing the cock bump back." And we did.

The ritual might be spreading, too! Clemson linebacker Ben Boulware sent me a message and photograph across social media on February 2, 2017, that showed him and a teammate celebrating with a cock bump in midair following a big play in the Tigers' national championship football victory over Alabama a month earlier.

I know it makes no sense to most people, but the game's little gestures mean a lot. The game is built on signs. Coaches signal in plays with a tip of the cap or a tug on their sleeve. I flashed signs to our pitchers—and even wore bright pink nail polish so they could see my fingertips. Many players across the league flash signs back to the dugout after they hit a base hit.

They are simple things but they give teammates a chance to celebrate with the player. At first, when I noticed other teams showing off some secret celebratory gesture, it bothered me. I thought, What are they doing? But when I got to Boston in 2013 I realized what was behind it. The true meaning was everyone on the bench was checked into that player's at-bat. A player got a hit, he flashed a sign back to the dugout, and everyone was fired up and shared in that hit.

Those signs are like high-fives. And everyone had a different version of a high-five.

My high-five just happened to be a "cock bump" that you got when you hit a home run.

CHAPTER 13

HIGH ANXIETY

11:24 P.M.

Cubs Lead, 6–3

My one-out home run in the top of the sixth inning had once again given us a three-run lead. My good friend and former Red Sox teammate Mike Napoli led off the bottom of the sixth inning for the Indians. My intention initially was to give Nap a quick hug before he got into the batter's box, but he looked dialed in and I didn't want to mess with his concentration. While in the batter's box, he said, "What's up, Rossy?" I replied, "What's up, Nap? I love you, buddy." And then we got back to work.

Jon Lester, who was also a teammate of Mike on the Red Sox during those two seasons, struck out Nap swinging on five pitches for the first out. Jose Ramirez grounded out to shortstop Addison Russell for the second out. Anthony Rizzo made a great stretch from first base on the throw as Ramirez nearly beat it out.

171

Brandon Guyer was next up, pinch-hitting for Lonnie Chisenhall, and he hit a two-out single between shortstop and third base into left field. Lester then fell behind in the count 3-1 to Rajai Davis, but got Rajai to hit a weak ground ball toward first base for the third out.

It was nice to get a quick, clean inning.

Andrew Miller started his second inning of relief against the top of our order in the seventh. Leadoff batter Dexter Fowler singled to right field for his third hit of the game. In a lefty-lefty matchup, Kyle Schwarber lined out to left field for the first out. With right-handed hitter Kris Bryant up next, Cleveland manager Terry Francona replaced Miller with the team's closer, right-hander Cody Allen. We had Andrew's number in Game Seven as he allowed 2 earned runs on 4 hits in 43 pitches.

Francona's move worked, though, as the Indians got a double play on a strike-'em-out-throw-'em-out. Allen struck out Kris swinging and catcher Roberto Perez threw out Dexter at second base on an attempted steal.

Lester remained solid in the bottom of the seventh as we protected our 6–3 lead. Coco Crisp flied out to short left field on his third pitch for the first out. Lester worked a full count on Roberto Perez before Perez walked and was replaced by pinch runner Tyler Naquin.

Then Carlos Santana hit a comebacker to the left side of the mound. I'm sure a lot of Cubs fans wondered how Jon would respond, given his troubles throwing to first base. It probably could have been a double-play ball, but Jon made sure to get one out, and threw the ball underhand to Rizzo. Two outs.

Jason Kipnis was up next. In the fifth, he'd singled in front of the plate, and I threw the ball past Rizzo at first, leading to that pair of Cleveland runs. Fortunately, nothing so dramatic happened this at-bat. This time Jon took matters into his own hands. He ended the inning with a strikeout of Jason on four pitches. Jon was doing exactly what he wanted to do with the baseball.

Allen sailed through a one-two-three inning in the top of the eighth on eleven pitches. Rizzo struck out swinging, Ben Zobrist grounded out to first base, and Addison Russell popped up to third base for the third out.

Even with a three-run lead and six outs away from a World Series title, as players we couldn't allow ourselves to think about clinching the victory. You are trying not to get ahead of yourself and so much emotion is riding on every pitch. That is why the play-offs are so draining emotionally and physically.

The bottom of the eighth inning started harmlessly enough as Lester struck out Francisco Lindor and Mike Napoli on eight pitches. But then came Jose Ramirez, who singled up the middle on a ball that shortstop Addison Russell couldn't handle. After the two-out hit, Joe Maddon elected to go to the bullpen. More precisely, he went to hard-throwing left-hander Aroldis Chapman in the hopes of a four-out save. It was the right time to get Jon out; his ball was losing some life and he had done his job.

Chappy, one of the hardest throwers in the major leagues, was traded to the Cubs from the New York Yankees in late July 2016 and he'd been a workhorse for us in the playoffs. Entering Game Seven, Chappy had thrown 238 pitches in 12 postseason appearances. That included an eight-out save on 42 pitches over 2.2 innings in our 3–2 win in Game Five. He also threw 20 pitches on one day's rest to get four outs in our 9–3 win in Game Six the previous night. Some were second-guessing that decision because he entered with a 7–3 lead in the bottom of the seventh with two on and two outs.

Chappy got Francisco Lindor to ground out for the third out, but he stayed in until the bottom of the ninth. He was replaced by Pedro Strop after a leadoff walk to Brandon Guyer and a 9–2 lead.

I hadn't caught Chapman since Game One of the National League Division Series against San Francisco on October 7, almost a month earlier.

With two outs and Ramirez on first base, Chappy threw Brandon Guyer a series of fastballs averaging 100.3 mph. Despite the heat, Guyer worked the at-bat to a 3-2 count. On Chapman's next heater, he socked a double to deep center field, scoring Ramirez and cutting into our lead at 6–4.

With right-handed hitter Rajai Davis up, my mindset hadn't changed when it came to my pitch selection. I mean, our guy threw 100 mph on every pitch and, in the back of my mind as a catcher, I don't want to get beat in a big situation with a pitcher's second- or third-best pitch. I thought we should stick with what I knew Chappy did best. If Rajai hit a home run off a slider, I'd never been able to forgive myself. So the scouting report had not changed. We wanted to pound Rajai with fastballs.

Chappy worked a 2-2 count on Davis and I thought I could get a fastball inside on him. But Davis dropped the bat head right on it and hit a line drive down the left-field line for a two-run home run that tied that game at 6–6.

Watching that ball go out was gut-wrenching. Chapman had only given up two home runs that entire 2016 regular season, and only nineteen in his six seasons in the majors. What were the chances he'd give one up now?

As I watched Davis's ball sail skyward, I was thinking, Hit the wall, hit the wall. No such luck. The game was now tied.

I know "Monday morning quarterbacks" will second-guess the pitch selection—they always do—especially in games that end in a loss. I also second-guessed myself. Why didn't I throw something else? Rajai had a good feel for the slider—which was Chappy's second-best pitch—that year from left-handers, but bad on changeups. Chappy had a good changeup and I probably should have gone with that. Of course I should have gone with that—I should have gone with anything but what I called. It's easy to think that way.

Looking back now, however, I wouldn't change a thing. I tell Cubs fans, we had to have a little drama, right? What fun would it have been to win by three or four runs. We wouldn't be able to say we were a part of one of the greatest World Series in history.

Anyway, we couldn't dwell on Rajai's home run. Our lead had vanished. We needed just one more out to get out of the inning. For a moment, it looked like it would never come. With the bases now clear, Coco Crisp singled between shortstop and third base.

Yan Gomes, who entered the game in the top of the eighth at catcher, was up next. We got the first two strikes with sliders, and then got him swinging at a fastball to end the inning.

Everyone tried to stay positive as we headed into the dugout. We were so high an inning earlier with the lead, and you could sense a letdown. That's only natural. All I knew was I had to have the at-bat of my life.

I led off the top of the ninth inning and worked a five-pitch walk off Cody Allen. I knew I had to get on base any way I could, but I never even considered that it might well be the last at-bat of my career. Even when Chris Coghlan replaced me as a pinch runner—which made it official, it was my last time competing in the major leagues—nothing really registered. I was focused on winning the game. It never occurred to me that I was walking off the field as a player for the last time. You know how your brain works when you're in the middle of competing? That's where I was locked.

I knew Game Seven would be a grind—it was my first Game Seven ever, so I was in a new element and I didn't have time to reminisce or play "what if." A lot of other people had reminisced for me, especially when you look at everything that was being said about me by the broadcast team. But I never had a chance to think that way.

We were in a tied game, 6–6.

. . . .

DAVID'S iPHONE JOURNAL
5/19/16

"Everyone on this plane is a professional, but not everyone is a pro!! Only one name on the marquee." —John Lackey

. . . .

Baseball is, of course, a game. As a game, it's supposed to be fun, across all levels—from Little League to pro baseball. Yes, there was tons of pressure in professional baseball—it was my job, and I had to perform. I am trying to provide for my family, just like the next guy. But everyone has to have fun at their job, too, right? If it isn't enjoyable, you're probably not going to be very good at it. I'm going to miss professional baseball for many reasons, and the fun I had playing is one of them.

It would sound pretty cinematic to say that, as I trotted off the field for the final time after my ninth-inning walk in Game Seven, all of the great memories from my fifteen-year career flashed before my eyes. The truth was that I was totally in the moment. Nostalgia would come later. Now, months later, I've had the chance to process some of these incredible memories. It seems like every day I think of something else that made me smile during my career. I couldn't resist sharing a few of the most cool, fun, and sometimes random moments and facts from my career.

Jersey Number. I wore six different jersey numbers at the major-league level—No. 40 with the Los Angeles Dodgers (2003–05), no. 29 with the Pittsburgh Pirates (2005), no. 9 with the San Diego Padres (2005), no. 26 with the Cincinnati Reds (2005–08), no. 8 with the Atlanta Braves (2009–12), and no. 3 with the Boston Red Sox (2008 and 2013–14) and Chicago Cubs (2015–16).

Number 8 was my favorite because of the success we experienced as a team in Atlanta, and it was my wife's softball number in high school, so she was pumped. When I signed with Boston in 2013, the team asked me what number I wanted. I really hadn't thought about it but said, "Oh, about eight?" They told me it wasn't available. I should have known. It was retired by the organization, having been worn by the great Carl Yastrzemski.

I was told nos. 3 and 5 were available and no. 3 clicked immediately in my mind. I liked that, in addition to myself, my family at that time had three others—wife, Hyla, and kids Landri and Cole. And the number 3 is like a half eight—that's how my brain works. But, as a backup catcher, I wasn't about to demand a certain jersey number from any organization. I was just happy I had a jersey.

Toughest Out. Lance Berkman, Todd Helton. These guys had it all, power to all fields, didn't give away one pitch, and I always felt like they knew what I was thinking. Todd was the most difficult in Colorado. I will never forget how he had a little grunt when he swung. It felt as if he were trying to cut the ball in half. The worst part about Helton was that you would work to get him to two strikes and your pitcher would make a perfect pitch and he would foul it off. He would do that till the pitcher made a mistake, and then he would hit a rocket somewhere.

Lance played in the Major Leagues fifteen years, was a National League All-Star six times, and won the 2011 World Series with the St. Louis Cardinals. He was a switch-hitter who averaged 30 home runs and had a .410 on-base percentage during his first twelve seasons. There weren't a whole lot of holes in his swing. I used to love when he would hit homers and set the bat down ever so gently because he knew it was gone.

Best Conversation at the Plate. I loved chatting with the umpires. I remember one with Bruce Froemming. Bruce umpired thirty-seven years in the major leagues, from 1971 until 2007, before he became the league's special assistant to the vice president on umpiring. He was one of the older umpires when I reached the big leagues, a real salty guy.

I was catching Paul Quantrill during spring training when I was with the Dodgers. Paul could hit a gnat's ass from the pitcher's mound at the tip of the plate. He threw a fastball and I was set up a little bit away, but the ball was almost middle of the plate. I caught it and Bruce called "Ball." I always tried to learn the umpire's names.

I said, "Hey, Bruce, where's that?"

And he said, "I had that ball down."

Next pitch was the same exact spot, maybe even right down the middle. I said, "Bruce, where's that." And he said, "What the heck is this, twenty questions? Throw the ball back." I tossed the ball back to Paul, but I nearly died of laughter. That line has stuck in my mind all of these years.

Another favorite umpire memory is of Joe West. As of 2016, Joe was the longest-tenured umpire in the league—he started in 1976 and joined the National League staff full-time in 1978. Joe could be a little rough around the edges, too, but I always liked him. He was brutally honest but a good umpire.

He did have a little bit of an ego and some showman in him. I was with the Red Sox in 2013 and one day we were playing the Yankees in Yankee Stadium. Jon Lester was on the mound, I was behind the plate, and right-handed hitter Vernon Wells was at-bat. Lester threw Vernon a cutter down and in. Vernon checked his swing, and as he did, he said, "Aww, my mind was telling me no." And for some reason R. Kelly popped in my head. I started to sing, "But my body, my body's telling me yes."

That's a lyric from the old R. Kelly song "Bump N' Grind." So I started to sing. And, without skipping a beat, Vernon started to sing the same song back to me. I mean Joe was like "What the . . . ?" He thought we were absolutely nuts. I loved that song in high school and it just popped into my head. Two guys at the plate singing R. Kelly to each other? It was a hilarious, almost unbelievable moment.

Best Conversation on the Mound. I have a few favorite memories of chats on the pitcher's mound, most of them with Jon Lester, of course. In 2014, when we both were with the Red Sox, Jon was dealing in a home game against the Oakland A's in early May. He'd struck out at least one batter in seven innings and struck out three in the third and the eighth innings. He was punching out tickets left and right, but he got a little sloppy with his pitches in the seventh or eighth inning. I felt like he let off the gas because the game was pretty much over and he had been cruising.

I had a sign I signaled to manager John Farrell when I thought the pitcher was done—I grabbed my uniform pant leg—so I grabbed my pant leg and walked out to the mound. First thing I said to Jon was—and it wasn't in a pleasant tone—"Are you done? Are you fucking done?" Jon was like, "No, no I'm fine." I screamed at him this time. "I will tell John you're done and he will get you the fuck out of here. We have guys in the bullpen if you are done. I'm not going to sit back here and catch this shit if you are not into it."

Of course, Lester got mad and said, *"No, I am not done."* I ran back behind home plate and he proceeded to strike out the side. He threw eight innings and finished with fifteen strikeouts.

. . . .

DAVID'S iPHONE JOURNAL
5/23/16

We have not been swinging the bats real well lately. We are not playing terrible, just can't get anything going offensively. I am playing more than normal and I am enjoying it. Can't seem to find a good workout program playing this much. At the end of a long road trip, two more with St. Louis. Lost tonight on a walk-off homer. Kids out of school Thursday and are meeting me in Chicago. So glad summer is here and can spend more time with them.

. . . .

Toughest Pitcher I Faced. Randy Johnson, hands down. The six-foot-ten lefty nicknamed "the Big Unit" was inducted into the Baseball Hall of Fame in 2015. With Randy, every time I saw a fastball or I was certain the next pitch was a fastball, I'd swing at 98 mph over my head. He just owned me.

The funny thing was, I got this thing for left-handers. I was good at hitting lefties but not Randy. Ted Lilly was another one. Ted played fifteen years in the major leagues and was a two-time All-Star. I could not hit his breaking ball. He was a pitcher who just baffled me. I would go up and look for his breaking ball, and he'd throw a fastball right down the middle of the plate and I'd just sit there and take it. It was awful.

However, the most defeated I had ever felt at the plate, simply because I was so overmatched, was when I faced the Yankees' Mariano Rivera. He carved me up like nobody's business. I watched strike one because I wanted to see what his cutter looked like. And then he threw me a front hip cutter, which I didn't even know was possible. I was still young enough in the league that I had never heard of a front hip cutter. I'm a right-handed batter and he threw the pitch at my left hip. I moved out of the way because I thought it was going to hit me and the pitch cut right across the middle of the plate.

The count was now 0-2 and I had no idea what pitch he'd throw next, but I knew I had to swing. I looked for another cutter, but, of course, he threw me high heat, probably 96 mph. I swung right through it, had no chance, and walked back to the dugout and said to myself, Whoa, okay. Now I see what all the hype is about this guy.

Favorite Pitcher to Face. I think I always had better results as a batter against pitchers I had caught. I had an advantage when I knew what their pitches would do rather than just seeing them for the first time.

I caught Zach Duke when we were with the Pittsburgh Pirates in 2005. I always saw the ball pretty well off Zach. Aaron Harang was one of my best buddies. Aaron was really dominant when we were together with the Cincinnati Reds, but he started to run out of juice later in his career so I managed to get the best of him a few times.

Favorite Stadium. On the road, San Francisco, by far. One of the game's best atmospheres, AT&T Park is just a beautiful place to play baseball. Situated on China Basin, a section of San Francisco Bay, it has the Coca-Cola Superslide, a big scoreboard, and a female announcer, Renel Brooks-Moon, who in 2016 was the only female public address announcer in Major League Baseball. She brought a different and cool vibe to the stadium.

As for home field, it's a tie between Wrigley Field and Fenway Park. There's so much atmosphere and history in those two spots.

Alias. When we went on the road, the name I used to sign into the hotel was Jake Taylor. It's the catcher's name from the movie *Major League.* Actor Tom Berenger played Jake Taylor in it. He was the old, salty catcher. "Come on, Dorn, get in front of the damn ball." It was easy to remember!

"Tallahassee." When fans I knew attended our games, they knew to shout "Tallahassee" when I walked by on the field to get my attention. It started when I was with Atlanta because a lot of people from my hometown of Tallahassee made the four-hour drive to watch games. I mean, nobody says "Tallahassee," so it was an easy way to get my attention.

When you stopped to sign autographs, it could be a process. It might take fifteen minutes to sign for everyone, and there were days I simply didn't have those fifteen minutes. But when somebody shouted "Tallahassee," I made sure to go out of my way to at least say hello. I started to tell my parents to tell people to say "Tallahassee" if they were coming to a game so I knew to look out for family and friends.

Perk I Will Miss. Man, it's just being catered to. I never picked up my equipment bags; everything already was there for you, ready to go. All the planning was done for you. I guess just the luxury of playing Major League Baseball, because everyone else takes care of you. But the competition, in my heart, is what I will miss the most, especially at the end of my career and the playoff atmospheres at Wrigley Field. There were fifty thousand people screaming for you, everyone watching on television. When I walked out of that stadium it was a pretty special feeling. I am really, really going to miss that.

◇

As that last career at-bat came and went in Game Seven, I wasn't thinking about these amazing memories that the game had given me. These thoughts had to wait . . . at least through a rain delay.

CHAPTER 14

RAIN DELAY

11:55 P.M.

Game Tied, 6–6

There may never have been a better-timed rain delay in the history of Major League Baseball. Thank you, Ernie Banks, Ron Santo, and other great Cubbies who watched from above, negotiated with the Big Guy, and created a little rain. Or as Ryan Dempster put it, Harry Caray spilled his Budweiser. The delay ended up being exactly what we needed.

Rain was in the forecast for Game 7, and it was expected to arrive around 11 p.m. It started to fall a little later than forecast, and we actually had a chance to snap the 6–6 tie in the top of the ninth inning prior to the delay. After I led off the inning with a five-pitch walk and was replaced by pinch runner Chris Coghlan, Jason Heyward grounded into a fielder's choice to force Coghlan out at second base. The Indians then brought in right-hander Bryan Shaw to replace Cody Allen.

Jason immediately stole second base and advanced to third base on a throwing error by Cleveland catcher Yan Gomes. With Jason

185

on third, Cleveland manager Terry Francona made a defensive move. Right fielder Brandon Guyer moved from right field to left field, and Michael Martinez entered the game in right—replacing Coco Crisp—to help prevent a sac fly that could score Heyward from third base due to Guyer's strong throwing arm.

Shaw, however, struck out Javier Baez when Javier fouled off a bunt attempt on a 3-2 count. Two outs. Dexter Fowler proceeded to ground out to shortstop. The Indians' Francisco Lindor made a great snag up the middle of the field to throw out Dexter and end the inning.

Though Chapman returned to the mound for the bottom of the ninth, I was out, owing to the pitch runner. Miggy Montero replaced me at catcher, while relievers Carl Edwards and Mike Montgomery started throwing in the bullpen. Chappy, who had lost some zip on his 100-plus mph fastball, relied on more sliders in the ninth. But he was effective and retired the top of the Indians' order on a fly-out (Carlos Santana), a swinging strikeout on a 97 mph fastball (Jason Kipnis), and a second fly-out (Francisco Lindor).

Game Seven was going to extra innings.

We were headed to the top of the tenth inning and "free baseball" but Mother Nature intervened. As the rain fell harder and the ground crew pulled the white tarps to cover the field, J-Hey immediately came to me and said, "Rossy, get everyone in the weight room, players only."

While Joe Maddon headed up the stairs to check on the weather, Jason motioned everyone into the weight room, just inside from the dugout, for a players-only meeting. It wasn't a big room, so everyone crowded in. I stood at the door and made sure all the fellas were there and to let a few curious coaches know the meeting was only for players.

. . . .

DAVID'S iPHONE JOURNAL
6/12/16

Just left ATL, lots of people came up from home to see me play. Was nice seeing a lot of my old friends. Some of my favorite years were there, great teams. Think I grew most as a player and person there. Had been awhile since my last hit, was nice for one to fall. Jon is pitching really well and continued that today. Forgot how hot it is here! Cole is with me in D.C. on a boys' trip. He rode with us on the team plane, and I think he loved it. We are going to have some good boy time while the girls are back in Tallahassee. My parents are there to help. We are all going to sightsee tomorrow, see if we can learn a little, too.

. . . .

The mic I wore during the game for the broadcast was still clipped to my jersey. But since I had no idea what was going to be said in the meeting—be it positive or negative—I covered the mic with my right hand and rubbed it to create the sound of friction. I didn't want anything to be leaked to the media or find its way onto the television broadcast. The last player who walked into the room was Chapman, and I saw immediately that he was crying. Like really, really upset.

Seeing Chappy like that really hit everyone hard. Seeing Chappy so emotional was particularly striking due to the language barrier. Chapman was born in Cuba and doesn't speak much English. (The Cubs hired a translator to help with Chappy's transition in the organization.) Everyone knew he was a great guy—he was our teammate—but he could be quiet on account of the language barrier, almost aloof. Seeing him in tears eliminated any question about how much he cared about the team and the moment.

When he walked in, I gave Chappy a big bear hug and whispered into his ear that we wouldn't be here without him.

It was true. Chapman had laid it on the line for us from the moment the Cubs acquired him from the Yankees in late July. He was a huge part of our late-year success. He had a 1.01 ERA with 16 saves in 28 appearances for us during the regular season, and threw 7.2 innings in the 2016 World Series. Compare that to the first half of the season, when he was pitching for the Yankees.

A big, imposing guy, he was a horse for us the whole season. I think he just ran out of gas in Game Seven. It happens to everyone. Your emotions are gone and everyone is exhausted. Now, in tears, he thought he had lost the game for us. Personally, when I saw Chappy like that, it made my desire to win even stronger, if only to do it for him. Everyone gave Chappy a big hug and it was like, "Screw that. Don't worry about it, brother. We are going to win."

Once Chappy arrived, I shut the door. Guys either stood or sat on the training room equipment. Even though it was a players-only meeting, I noticed that Tim Buss, our strength and conditioning coach, was near the back sitting with his head down. Nobody minded Tim was there, though. Jason stood in a corner of the room and started the meeting. It was his idea. Jason is a quiet guy but he's enormously respected by his teammates. His struggles in 2016 and a big contract had dominated a lot of media, but the guy never changed, and the way we viewed him and his importance to the team didn't, either. When Jason talked, everyone listened.

At a few other moments in the playoffs Jason had considered speaking to the team, but the timing never felt right. But, at that moment in Game Seven, with the rain delay and everything that had happened to us—after we had been four outs away from winning the Series before the Indians tied the game and forced extra innings—Jason felt the guys needed to hear what he had to say.

Here we were in the biggest moment of the year and a guy who could have checked out instead was standing up to bring us together. *That* is being a good teammate.

Jason's wasn't a fire-and-brimstone speech. It was direct, but personal, from the heart and with plenty of passion. Jason reminded everyone that, as players and as the Cubs team, all of us had overcome challenges during the season. We had faced obstacles but took all of them in stride. We had overcome every obstacle to reach this point in Game Seven, and that was why we were the best team in Major League Baseball. We'd won 103 games in the regular season and 113 games total.

Jason reminded the guys not to change a thing once the game resumed. He said there were other people involved in the Cubs organization who had their hand in our success. But, at the end of the day it was us who had to overcome everything. Nobody else. There was so much going on during the playoffs and the World Series, too. It was such a busy time. Players didn't hang out together as much because everyone had families and friends visiting. You'd practice, shower, and got the heck out of there. Our cocoon was so tight during the regular season, but I think with some of the distractions of the postseason, that togetherness and closeness started to creep out.

After all the distractions, Jason's players-only meeting brought everyone back to center. This was about *us*. It wasn't about anything or anybody else. Jason reminded us to go back out and compete for your brother next to you and have fun.

It wasn't long, but Jason's message made a big impact. A few other players made some comments—quick, keep-your-head-up type things. Everyone was positive, upbeat. The rain delay lasted only seventeen minutes. Somebody knocked on the door and everyone returned to the dugout to get loose. Jason's message was in our minds.

He reminded us we were winners.

◇

What makes a good teammate? What actions can a teammate make to pull his fellow players together in good and bad times? Jason's players-only speech, I believe, showed off a lot of the necessary qualities. It showed that, as teammates, we trusted Jason's judgment. It showed that we communicated as a team and believed in each other. Everyone was focused on the ultimate goal.

Creating a perfect team is extremely difficult, because players come and go all the time. With the collective bargaining agreement and free agency, a lot of players are on the move. Guys get released, traded, promoted, and demoted. Players rarely control their own destiny. To find that mix of twenty-five players who really care about each other and know how to motivate each other and learn how to work together in a high-stress environment—and then to win on top of it—is not easy. If it were, every team would have a winning record.

When I was playing for the Braves, I remember being in Phil Falco's office one day in the middle of the season. Phil was the strength and conditioning coach for the Braves at the time and, for whatever reason, we started to talk that day about what habits make a winner, what habits make a good teammate.

The weight room is a great sanctuary for players. It's off-limits to the media, so players can head back there to relax, make a personal telephone call, shoot the breeze, stretch, get a workout in, or just talk about life, baseball, anything. Phil had a big white dry-erase board in his office and, off the cuff, that day we started a list of words and phrases that we thought made a winner and made a good teammate. Words and phrases like *hard worker, unselfishness, honesty,* etc. Phil wrote them in big, bold letters so all the players could see them when they came by his office. Other players like Eric O'Flaherty and Eric Hinske got into the act, too, and we'd all sit with Phil and brainstorm the right mix of characteristics that made up winners and good teammates.

From there it took off, and it became a game. It was a positive, fun thing and nobody's feelings got hurt. We listed the words and phrases and we judged each player individually, awarding or subtracting points on each criterion. We'd bring a guy in and start going down the list! We had a ten-point scale and needed a calculator to keep score.

Martin Prado was one of the greatest teammates I ever had. He worked his tail off when we were together with the Braves. He was the same dude every day. He didn't ride the emotional roller coaster and he did everything right. He always got high scores. But even

Martin tried to dispute some of the criteria when we judged him. It was fun. For instance, a player might have said he worked hard and gave himself a score of 10, but everybody in the room that day may have only given him a 7. We would tell him he wasn't being honest with himself. That was the biggest word on the list, *honesty.*

We always wondered why more guys weren't truthful about who they are. I had a T-shirt made that said, "Be honest with yourself." It had a picture of Falco on the front of it and we handed the shirts out to players. (Some of those shirts are still in circulation around the league.) When a player walked in, he might say he had prepared well, but we'd answer, "Dude, you're not prepared enough. Be honest with yourself." Another guy might have said, "No, I am working hard but I'm just not working smart."

Eric O'Flaherty was one of the hardest workers and didn't have many flaws but he was always the last person to stretch, so we would deduct points for not being on time and not being prepared. Another player would come in and we'd bash him about his eating habits and needle him a little: "Dude, you're fat, you're overweight." Obviously you don't play at this level without being in shape, but we were pushing each other to be even more so. We had guys on the Braves who were ripped and shredded, and I always wanted to look like that, too. But I had to ask myself, Am I really working hard enough to achieve that goal? I'd take off my shirt in the weight room and grab my love handles. I'd jump up and down and tell my teammates, "Look, dude, look at my fat, just jiggling up and down." When it came to grading a player's body composition, the player had to take off his shirt in the weight room. Phil turned off all the lights, with the exception of a few strobe lights, and the player jumped up and down in front of the mirrors so everyone could see their fat jiggle. We'd shine those strobe lights on their fat. Locker room antics.

One of the first phrases on Phil's board was "Are you a hard worker?" What did it mean to work hard? We talked about how early guys got to the ballpark, who took extra ground balls. Just because you are the first one there and the last to leave doesn't make you a hard worker. Joe Maddon would say that was the guy who had no life.

The key to working hard is working smart. A player can work hard, but what if he's doing too much, like taking 10,000 swings in the batting cage when he only needs 100 swings? In that case, a player isn't working smart.

Another phrase was "Game preparation." What did a player do when he was done with batting practice? Did he take care of himself? Did he do all the things necessary to get himself physically and mentally prepared for the game?

The most important thing was that we were able to get our point across without upsetting anyone or losing a relationship with that player. We were getting true, honest feedback from our teammates. Here's what it means to be a winner. It was done in good humor, but in the end the experience gave the teammates some concrete feedback on ways to improve themselves. It helped everyone on the team understand what each other was thinking. It brought a sense of accountability to the team.

• • • • • • • • • • • • • • •

DAVID'S iPHONE JOURNAL
7/23/16

If you want to know what's wrong with a pitcher, look at where the fastball is going!! Really feel like we are not a team right now. Feel like I should say something. Wondering if I'm getting too distracted with all this "last year" bullshit?! I am having a blast with my family though.

. . . .

The idea of studying what it means to build a winning team was brought to another level last year when one of my favorite base-ball execs, Ben Cherington, the general manager who helped direct the Red Sox to the 2013 World Series title, created a survey that he sent to a number of players. It collected anonymous responses from players for a study that Ben undertook to identify concepts that improve work culture.

Ben wanted to understand more about what players thought mattered in the clubhouse. He wanted us to be honest about our responses—and not just tell him what we thought because he had been the GM of the Red Sox. I thought it was a good idea and really showed that character mattered.

When I signed with the Red Sox, Ben admitted he had weighed both tangible attributes and more intangible factors. I had hit above .250 in three of my four seasons with the Braves. Ben believed I'd play good defense, that I'd hit left-handed pitching, and that Fenway Park was a good fit for me offensively because of the park's dimensions. But Boston also wanted to build a better culture. The Red Sox had hired a new manager in John Farrell and made other moves to help restore a level of professionalism and energy in the clubhouse. They brought in players who would aid in that goal. Guys with good character, guys who'd proven they were winners. I had played briefly with the Red Sox previously, in 2008, so management knew me. But they didn't know I'd drive the conversation in the clubhouse quite the way I did during my two seasons in Boston.

The 2013 Red Sox team had so many great players and leaders. Much like Jason Heyward's impromptu players-only meeting in Game Seven of the 2016 World Series, David Ortiz rounded us up for a rare pep talk in the Boston dugout during the sixth inning of Game Four of the 2013 World Series against the St. Louis Cardinals. The score was tied 1–1. "Big Papi" didn't say much, but what he said was important. During that game in the Series, he wanted to remind everyone that, hey, don't take this for granted. It's not every day you get to play in the World Series. He reminded everyone how special the opportunity was. David said he'd been on teams that had more talent but had never made the Series. So he challenged everyone to leave it on the field, and when David spoke, you listened.

There's no clear-cut formula to building a winning culture. Each organization has its own philosophy and way of doing business. And it's difficult as a professional athlete because there are so many things going on in your life outside the clubhouse, whether you're twenty-five, thirty, or thirty-five years old. In addition to your day-to-day performance, you're dealing with your family, your contract status, trying to stay healthy. You're trying to hit .280 but only hitting .220. It's easy to get so wrapped up in yourself and what you're doing in your life that you fail to understand that you're still part of a team.

To be a great teammate, a player has to have a good work ethic, he has to be durable, he has to be mentally tough, he has to have perseverance, and he has to have talent. It has to be a player who can lead a group, but also can take care of himself to make sure that his job gets done. It's difficult to find a baseball player or a professional athlete in any sport who excels at all those things, which is why extraordinary teammates are so hard to find.

. . . .

DAVID'S iPHONE JOURNAL
8/8/16

Just finished road trip to Oakland! What a week!!
Let me tell you all about it! Baseball has been
going great! We have won 7 in a row. During that
span we had another few crazy comebacks against
Seattle and Miami. I think the Seattle game really
jump-started us. We were down 6 in the third after
starting a guy from AAA for no reason. Bullpen
was amazing and I got to catch Chapman for the
first time. We put Woody in left field again and he
made a great catch. Think that was our first walk-
off of the year, felt good. We have been rolling
since then, 7 in a row, with another walk-off 3
days later vs. the Marlins. The trip to Oakland was
amazing! Lester flew us to Pebble Beach to stay
the night and golf, had a blast and played well.
Then Saturday after the day game we went to
see Kenny Chesney in concert at the new 49er's
stadium. While all that was going on we swept the
A's. Off day yesterday took kids to Six Flags water
park all day. Kids had a blast and I got blistered.

. . . .

We returned to the dugout following Jason's speech during
the seventeen-minute rain delay and everyone started to get loose.

Everyone was fired up. Kyle Schwarber, a left-handed hitter who was scheduled to lead off the top of the tenth inning, came up to me in the dugout and said, "Rossy, I'm going to back off the plate and this guy [Bryan Shaw] is going to throw me a cutter. If it starts in the middle, I am going to go deep." Kyle said it as calm and matter-of-factly as could be. That's just the way he is.

Anthony Rizzo was running up and down the dugout, saying things like "We're the best team in baseball" and "This is our game, boys." Rizz was at the bat rack getting his batting gloves on and I was in the middle of the dugout. I shouted to him, "Rizz, it's not how many times you get knocked down!" and he shouted back, "It's how many times you get back up, baby!" Now he was really fired up, screaming and running around.

We went out in the bottom of the tenth inning and it was boom, boom, boom. The focus was back on.

All thanks to Jason's speech. And a well-timed rain delay.

CHAPTER 15

CUBS WIN, CUBS WIN

12:47 A.M.

Game Tied, 6–6

After seventeen minutes and one pep talk, we were ready to roll.

Our numbers two, three, and four hitters were due up in the top of the tenth against Indians reliever Bryan Shaw. Shaw had thrown fourteen pitches in the bottom of the ninth prior to the delay and Kyle Schwarber, as he promised in the dugout minutes earlier, went into his at-bat aggressive to lead off the tenth.

The left-handed-hitting Schwarber had hit .412 in the World Series—this, after sitting out nearly the whole season while recovering from two ligament tears in his left knee. With the infield shift in place, Schwarber singled on the second pitch to right field. It was two feet to second baseman Jason Kipnis's left but Kyle hit the ball so hard Kipnis didn't even have time to react.

In the dugout, we felt a jolt of energy—here we go, leadoff guy on! We were at our best all year when that leadoff guy got on base. As a catcher, I knew it was always the most important out of each inning.

Albert Almora entered as a pinch runner for Schwarber. Albert made a great read on a long fly ball to center field from Kris Bryant, who came up second. Albert tagged up and advanced to second base to beat the throw from Indians center fielder Rajai Davis.

With one out and a runner in scoring position, Indians manager Terry Francona decided to give Anthony Rizzo a free pass and Shaw intentionally walked him after a meeting on the mound. Now we had runners on first and second.

Up next was left-handed-hitting Ben Zobrist, who had won a World Series ring with the Kansas City Royals in 2015 and signed a four-year, $56 million deal with the Cubs in December 2015. So far in the game he was 0-for-4 with a run scored. But now he delivered.

Zobrist laced a 1-2 cutter off Shaw for an opposite-field RBI double down the third base line to score Almora from second base.

The Fox television broadcast caught the emotion of the moment as Zobrist jumped, waved his clenched right fist in the air, and lost his helmet as he landed on second base. Rizz, now at third, placed his hands on top of his helmet and mouthed, "Oh my God."

Cubs 7, Indians 6.

Shaw then issued another intentional walk, this one to Addison Russell, to load the bases with one out.

Left-handed Miguel Montero, who entered the game in the bottom of the ninth when I was lifted for a pinch runner, followed with a ground-ball single to left field on a 1-1 cutter. Rizzo crossed the plate, bases were still loaded.

Score: 8–6.

In trouble, Francona opted for the pitching change. Right-hander Trevor Bauer, the Indians' starter and loser in Game Two and Game Five, entered in relief and struck out Jason Heyward for the second out. Then he got Javier Baez to fly out to deep center field for the third out.

We had the lead back.

. . . .

DAVID'S iPHONE JOURNAL
8/12/16

"Winners focus on winning, losers focus on winners." What an atmosphere tonight! Was probably the hottest game of the year and the guys kept pushing. Great team win vs. the Cardinals. Puts us 13 games up. Wrigley was rocking! I'm exhausted!

. . . .

Hard-throwing right-hander Carl Edwards Jr., a forty-eighth-round selection in the 2011 major-league draft, was on the mound for us to start the bottom of the tenth. He had struck out the side in a relief appearance in the top of the sixth inning in Game Three.

My heart was racing. As a player, you are trying to stay calm and be as normal as possible, which is very difficult in that environment. The nerves are high and you are just so anxious and it's like you can barely breathe. Now Edwards recorded the first two outs in quick succession: a strike from Mike Napoli and a ground-out by Jose Ramirez. Again, you never want to get ahead of yourself. In baseball, the third out is always the most difficult. That was the case in Game Seven, too.

Carl fell behind Brandon Guyer 3-0 and walked Guyer two pitches later. That brought a mound visit from our pitching coach Chris Bosio with Rajai Davis at the plate. Rajai, of course, hit the two-run home run in the eighth inning to tie the game. We allowed Guyer to advance to second base without a throw on Carl's first pitch to Davis. Davis came up big again, smacking a single to center field that drove in Guyer.

Cubs 8, Indians 7.

My heart was pounding! I was worried about Rajai stealing second. At that point, a bloop single would tie it again. Could we really give up two leads in a single game?

Joe Maddon went to the bullpen and brought in left-hander Mike Montgomery to face right-handed hitter Michael Martinez. As Montgomery trotted to the mound, every second felt like an eternity. The crowd was going nuts but you almost become numb to the noise because you are so focused on the task at hand. There was so much pressure on every pitch.

Mike's first pitch was a curveball. Strike one. On the second pitch, Martinez—with Davis running—tapped a slow roller to third baseman Kris Bryant. Off the bat the ball looked like it might be an infield hit.

Kris Bryant had other plans.

Kris charged toward the ball near the mound and fielded it cleanly. Though his front foot slipped slightly when he planted to throw, Kris made a clean exchange and zipped it over to Rizzo at first base, beating out Martinez by a good three strides.

And with that, Rizzo stuffed the ball in his back pocket and threw his glove in the air, and the celebration started.

The Cubs were World Series champions for the first time in 108 years!

As Fox game announcer Joe Buck said, "What a game. What a Series. What a night."

• • • • • • • • • • • • • • •

DAVID'S iPHONE JOURNAL
9/19/16

Crazy weekend! We clinched on a loss by Cardinals but Miggy hit a walk-off home run the next day that started the party just right! One of the best celebrations I had been a part of, they had a DJ in our locker room. At one point there was so much beer and champagne being poured on my head I couldn't breathe. It was so cold, gave me brain freeze from the outside. Only down spot was not having family here. They are very busy at home with school and activities but are coming up this Wednesday for the weekend and back full time for playoffs. More parties to come.

• • • • • • • • • • • • • • •

I was a tad slow out of the gate following the third out. As I climbed over the dugout railing, left leg first, my cleat got caught. But I made it over cleanly and rushed the field to join my teammates. Honestly, it was a blur. I remember embracing Kris Bryant, Anthony Rizzo, and Jason Heyward. Kris was crying and I remember him thanking me and telling me he loved me.

Appearing from out of nowhere, World Series T-shirts and caps were being passed around. Carl Edwards Jr. ran around the field with a "Cubs Win" flag above his head. There were cameras everywhere. It was just a cool, emotional experience.

The game had so many ups and downs. I was totally spent after the game. With glassy, moist eyes, I tried my best to explain my feelings to Ken Rosenthal of Fox when he interviewed me live on the field following the game and asked me what it was like. "What a group of winners, what a group of resilient winners," I managed to say. "These guys have never quit. They've answered every challenge all year long. When you just want to crumble when that ball goes over the fence, these guys fight back and continue to have good at-bats and play their game." I told him, "I am so happy for these guys and I am just glad they took me on this journey."

My self-deprecating humor kicked in when Ken told me I looked almost stunned when I rounded the bases after I hit my solo home run in the sixth inning. "You would be stunned, too, if you had my swing," I joked.

At that point, manager Joe Maddon and I shared an emotional hug as he repeatedly patted me on the back with his right hand, which held a World Series T-shirt. Ken's last question was about my retirement and my family and the prospect of spending more time with them. He asked if that was on my mind. "It wasn't. It was staying in the moment. When we won, my first thoughts were on my wife, what a great way, what a great journey these guys took me on. I am just so proud of these guys. The city of Chicago deserves it. With these guys, with these guys . . ."

I was babbling at that point. Suddenly, as I was in midsentence, Anthony Rizzo, on my right, and Jason Heyward, on my left, came up from behind me and lifted me on their shoulders and carried me off. Can you believe it? The backup catcher gets carried off after Game Seven? That just doesn't happen anywhere but in the movies. (Are there any movies about backup catchers?)

I high-fived a couple of my teammates as they toted me toward our dugout along the first base line. I blew a kiss to the crowd with my right hand. It was such an emotional moment, a "Rudy" moment, something I never expected. I'll remember for the rest of my life this moment when I was literally carried off the field and into retirement as a World Series champion.

But one thing was a little awkward, if I'm being honest. As I told Tom Verducci of *Sports Illustrated,* when I was on their shoulders I didn't know what to do with my hands! Do I wave, do I point, do I blow kisses? It was so surreal and incredible.

A few minutes later, the trophy presentation took place in our clubhouse, where everyone was ready to pop champagne and celebrate. On a stage near the wall stood Fox announcer Kevin Burkhardt, MLB commissioner Rob Manfred (standing next to the Commissioner's Trophy), Cubs owner and executive chairman Tom Ricketts, Executive of Baseball Operations Theo Epstein, President of Business Operations Crane Kenny, General Manager Jed Hoyer, and Manager Joe Maddon.

Theo, Crane, and Jed unveiled the "Cubs Win" flag as Kevin made the introductions. The commissioner lifted the Commissioner's Trophy off the table next to him and presented it to Tom Ricketts, saying it was an honor to present it to the Cubs and adding how historic it was. "Your fans waited one hundred and eight years and you delivered in style," he said.

Tom lifted the trophy above his head as we cheered. When asked by Fox announcer Burkhardt what it felt like to hold the trophy, Tom said, "It's incredible. I just think about so many millions of people giving so much love and support towards this team for so many years. To finally pay them back . . ." And when Kevin followed up with another question on how it felt, Tom shouted as he looked toward everyone in the clubhouse, "Hey, how does it feel to be world champions? It feels pretty good."

Tom passed the trophy to Theo, who lifted it skyward. When asked how he was surviving the heart-attack game as he watched from the stands near our dugout, Theo said, "This is fitting that it has to be done with one of the best games of all time. It's unbelievable. What a testament to our players, their grit."

The trophy was handed off to Joe Maddon, the Cubs' fifty-third manager since 1908—and who was ready to celebrate with goggles around the top of his world champions cap. "It's the baby, it's your first baby," Joe said as he cradled the trophy. When asked what he was most proud of accomplishing, Joe said—as somebody threw a World Series champion hat toward the stage—"You just heard them say we never quit. I am really proud of the attitude and the culture that we have created here obviously. I think it's something that carries for many, many years to come."

After the speeches, Ben Zobrist was awarded the Most Valuable Player of the Series with a nice trophy and a fiftieth-anniversary Chevrolet Camaro.

Now, finally: It was time to party!

One of the highlights was bullpen catcher Chad Noble, who stripped down to a Speedo bathing suit as the champagne sprayed. As for me, I kept the champagne celebration short and sweet.

I wanted to get out to the field to see my wife and kids.

It wasn't about me or my family when I got out of bed nearly sixteen hours earlier in our hotel suite. But at this moment it was all about them.

. . . .

DAVID'S iPHONE JOURNAL
9/9/16

Had off day yesterday in Houston, love the Galleria mall! Took a few guys to my favorite sushi spot Uchi. Have a noon game tomorrow then Lester is flying us to TCU–Arkansas game. Can't wait for that. We have been playing very good except vs. Milwaukee. Think it's hard to get up to play them. Lester has been pitching great, so glad he is having a good year. Long road trip, need to play well here and St. Louis. Got a big lead in division, should close out soon. Harper is going to start walking really soon. She is standing all by herself, uh oh!

. . . .

When Game Seven ended, Hyla, Landri, and Cole (who still didn't feel well) and other families waited in the stands to be escorted to the tunnel near our locker room. The bottom bowl of Progressive Field still was packed with Cubs fans thirty minutes after the game. It probably was around forty-five minutes or so when I first spotted Hyla and the kids waiting outside the locker room. I grabbed Cole and we headed into the dugout to sit. We tried to take a couple of family photographs on the field, but Cole wasn't up to it. I took him into the training room to get him something to drink and have him lie down to rest, while Hyla and Landri waited in the dugout as the rain returned, this time in monsoon-like fashion. While I was being pulled in what seemed like one hundred different directions by interview requests, Hyla, in the dugout, started talking to a guy who sat down next to her and introduced himself. It was Eddie Vedder, lead singer of Pearl Jam. And lifelong Cubs fan.

Eddie gave me an incredible shout-out during the seventh-inning stretch of Game Five of the World Series at Wrigley Field. I mean, that was such an emotional game for me. We were down three games to one in the Series. We had lost the previous night 7–2 and were on the brink of elimination. It was my last game at Wrigley and potentially the last game of my career.

The guys had been feeling pretty down when we walked into our locker room after Game Four. But as I got undressed, I heard someone slam their glove in their locker. I had no idea who it was but this overwhelming feeling to say something came over me. I battled that voice for a second and then I let it go. I was like, "No, we are not going to do that." I wanted to put things in perspective. I was like, "Hey, we have Game Five tomorrow at Wrigley Field. This is the World Series. Every baseball player in the world would trade places with us to get a chance to play in that game tomorrow, right?" Plus, I reminded them, "Daddy's in the lineup tomorrow. We are fine. I will take care of everything."

All season that was my way of lightening moments. I stole that from Dustin Pedroia. He would always call himself Daddy when he would start talking trash, and it always made me laugh. I only got to play every few days, but I always made it a point to say, "We don't lose when Daddy plays!" The guys had spent so much time calling me Grandpa, but I couldn't go there. I had to be Daddy. And it worked out for us.

When I was lifted from the game for pinch hitter Miguel Montero in the bottom of the sixth inning in Game Five, it was a tough, emotional moment. I went to Lester, hugged him, and told him I loved him. I went back into the locker room to change and gather my emotions.

As it happens, Eddie Vedder was scheduled to sing "Take Me Out to the Ball Game" during the seventh-inning stretch, one of the cool traditions at Wrigley. When I walked back in the dugout, everyone looked at me and said, "Dude, Eddie Vedder just dedicated the whole seventh-inning stretch to you." I was like, "What?" Eddie had thanked Theo Epstein, Tom Ricketts, and Joe Maddon before he mentioned me. "There's one guy in particular I want to sing my butt off for. He's number three, he's behind the plate, he may retire, but he'll never quit. Mr. David Ross, I'd like to belt this one out for you. It's his last game at Wrigley, let's sing it for him."

I really didn't hear what was said or what went on but I was totally blown away. I had gotten to know Eddie a little bit—he was a regular around Wrigley Field when he wasn't on the road with his band—and he's really a down-to-earth guy, a genuine human being. Everyone knows who Eddie Vedder is. I walked to the top of the dugout and tipped my cap Eddie's way in the announcer's booth. To say my name and honor me was a huge compliment. So, how cool and surreal is it that Hyla talked to Eddie about life, baseball, the Cubs, and children in our dugout after Game Seven?

I don't think we left Progressive Field until 3 a.m. It wasn't a great experience for family members as everyone waited in the dugout on the players. Plus the sky opened up and it was pouring rain. We were being pulled in so many different directions that it was a chore just to break away and shower. While Landri was fine and mingled with friends, Cole was tired and lay in Hyla's lap most of the time.

Finally, everyone boarded the buses to head to Cleveland Hopkins International Airport for our charter flight to Chicago. En route to the airport on Interstate 71 south, a truck that had a mobile billboard sign pulled up in the lane next to the buses.

It displayed a huge, glowing white and blue "Cubs Win" flag.

CHAPTER 16

HOMECOMING

4 A.M.

A fter 108 years of waiting, our charter flight from Cleveland to Chicago carried the holy grail of professional baseball.

The Commissioner's Trophy.

Thirty pounds of sterling silver, the two-foot-tall trophy is covered with thirty metal flags on it, one for each major-league team, and a gold-stitched baseball. It's absolutely beautiful. The best part of our forty-five-minute flight from Cleveland airport to O'Hare International Airport on the northwest side of Chicago wasn't the party. While there was plenty of music and beverage consumption on board the flight, everyone was exhausted, too. The best part was that we finally had a chance to exhale.

In our family, Cole still wasn't feeling well and he was laid out across a row of seats, asleep. Landri sat near the back of the plane with one of her friends, wide awake! I'm sure they enjoyed watching the festivities.

Everyone, myself included, was all smiles as we passed around the Commissioner's Trophy. I tweeted a picture of myself with the trophy and said, "Look what the boys got me for my retirement." While I'd held the trophy before—the first time was 2013 with the Boston Red Sox—this time was the best feeling in the world.

. . . .

DAVID'S iPHONE JOURNAL
9/28/16

Listen to your teammates, they will tell you the truth. What a crazy weekend! Let me start by saying how much love these guys give me! I'm going to miss them. Friday the Cubs did a video for me and a ceremony with my family. Couldn't hold back the tears! They gave me some cool gifts, home plate from NH, jersey I hit 100th HR, and #3 from score board. Sunday, last home game, SNBB, and I'm catching. What a night!! I got a standing O my first two at-bats and went deep after the second one. What an amazing feeling! Later, with two quick outs in the 7th, Joe comes out to take Jon out, or so I thought. He tells me, "I've never done this but you're out of the game." I was so confused, and then all my teammates start patting me on the head and shoulders. I pulled my mask down, so no one would see me starting to cry, and headed to dugout. Hugs from my teammates and coaches, another curtain call, we win, what a night. Side note,

my parents were sitting right behind home plate,
three rows up! Thanks to the best, Vijay!

. . . .

I established a reputation in the major leagues as a good teammate. I had some missteps along the way, but I learned through my
experiences—good and bad—the habits of good teammates and the
importance of being invested in others. And the difference over the
final eight years of my career was how intentional I was about it.
I did a lot of thinking about the different ingredients that go into
winning, to the point where I almost had it down to a formula.
I understood how important preparation was. I understood how
important relationship-building was. I understood the importance
of certain conversations away from the playing field. I understood
how important it was to have someone who could hold the team
accountable, for doing all the little things.

I thought about how I could create all those different ingredients and actively create those in other people. I always tried to keep
an eye on my teammates and how they affected the whole team. All
those little moments throughout the season, the simple conversations, the team dinners, were intended to foster relationships that
helped create a winning environment. But being a good teammate
doesn't guarantee winning. Good teams have a lot of moving parts
that work in unison. While teams are only as good as their superstar players—talent still wins in most environments—character is
a key ingredient to an improved working culture.

There has actually been a fair amount of academic and socio-
logical research done on the subject of being a good teammate. As

that phrase has been thrown around about me, I've had a good deal of time to think about what it all means. Here are a few characteristics of being a good teammate, from that research, and examples of how they helped me during my career.

Humility

Let me start by addressing the irony of talking about the importance of humility . . . in a book all about me. But I say this all the time: Selfishness is the root of evil in baseball and most other walks of life. Selfishness takes everybody down. If you're consumed with yourself, then you're not going to do what's best for the team. Whether it's getting a guy over from first to second base or having to take a bunch of pitches for the next guy, grinding out pitchers, giving yourself up for others is the ultimate act of humility.

Every team needs a rock star or two. If Albert Pujols and Mike Trout don't produce, the Angels are going to be terrible, right? Same with us. If Rizzo and Kris Bryant don't produce, we're not going to be very good. But those guys will never win without the team. The lineup works right when every dude gets on board with the plan.

We had a situation in Boston where the Red Sox signed a free agent. At that time, we were a team that grinded out at-bats. Suddenly this new guy comes in—he was making good money—and just did his own thing. I remember once when he came to the plate with the bases loaded against a pitcher who was struggling to find the strike zone. Instead of being patient, our guy went up and swung at the first pitch and grounded out. It was the wrong mindset. It was a selfish mindset.

If you're only worried about your stats, everyone will see your true colors. That was me in Cincinnati. I learned a huge lesson.

Honesty

I had a situation with a good buddy, Mike Napoli, in Boston in 2013. Mike played every day and this guy really grinded. He was suffering from an injured foot and, I believe, got a cortisone shot that day. It was a Sunday game that I started and Mike and a few other guys were in the locker room watching football. We had clenched the division two nights before and Nap played every day. He deserved to relax and do whatever he wanted to get ready for the playoffs. I remembered coming off the field a couple of times and thought, Man, where's Nap? I don't know why I noticed it and I don't know why it drove me crazy, but I thought, Where's Nap? I started to get hot and after a few innings I couldn't stand it.

I always felt that holding my emotions in made me a bitter person. So I walked into the locker room and then up another set of stairs to the weight room, where Mike was hanging out with a few other guys who were not playing that day. I saw them watching football. So, internally, I was pissed, but my initial thought wasn't to make a big deal about it. I grabbed a Red Bull from the refrigerator and then, as I started to head back to the field, I couldn't help myself. I said, "Hey, man, I just want to tell you something. I'm out there supporting you every day that you play and I don't appreciate that I'm playing today and you don't have my back."

As I walked out I immediately second-guessed myself and thought, You've got to be kidding me. Why did I do that? I'm just burning bridges. The next thing I knew, Mike was back on the bench during the game. Afterward, he apologized and told me he was hurting and the team doctor told him to take it easy. But he said he should've been on the bench and not upstairs watching football. Our relationship grew that day, in part because I was honest with him and he allowed me to be that.

We had a similar incident in Chicago in 2016. It was an extra-inning game in late September and there were a bunch of pitchers in the locker room, including Rob Zastryzny, a rookie, a great kid. Former Cubs pitcher Rick Sutcliffe was in there, too.

I was on the bench and I looked around as it got emptier and emptier. You don't always need a bunch of guys cheering in the dugout, but on a night like that you need all the help you can get. I said, "Screw this. The dugout is empty. We're out here playing and we don't have any support."

I walked into the locker room and let loose. "You know, we're out here grinding and you guys are in here shooting the shit. Rookie, Rob Z, get your ass out here. You get your ass out here. Veterans, you can do whatever the hell you want but we're trying to win a baseball game."

Sutcliffe told me afterward it was the coolest thing he'd ever seen. I didn't like doing that, and it's not something that made me feel cool. Every time I did it I got emotional because I knew that the situation wasn't right. And when something isn't right, I have to say something. That's honest.

Reliability

Be the same person every day. That's a big saying in baseball. Joe Maddon loves to say, "Okay, be the same guy. Don't carry yesterday into today." I talked to Hyla about it a lot. When I walked into our locker room I felt I had to bring the energy, even when I was having a bad day.

If you're consistent in your daily routine and in your personality, it makes it easier to focus. To manage a long baseball season, you must prepare and break down each day and be consistent in your approach, no matter who your opponent is on a given day.

That's why my routine included saying "hello" to everyone when I got to the park that day. It was my way of checking in and getting ready. Everyone knew it was coming, even the security guards, Steve and Melvin!

Communication

Communication can be positive or negative. Everyone makes mistakes. When a player made a mistake, I thought it was important to lift him up.

Jon is one of those guys who know how to work. He prepares every day and builds for his start every fifth day. Jon's a little bit like a robot until he's done with his work. One consequence of this was that when he pitched and somebody booted a ball behind him, his body language might suggest he was upset with that player. The risk was that the player might think Jon didn't like him or the player might become scared to play behind Jon.

Early in the 2015 season I told him, "Hey, man, listen. You're going to be here five, six years and I am outta here in one more year, maybe, unless they get rid of me sooner than that. But you have to make an effort to get to know these guys so they don't think you're a scary human being." I mean, he's a big teddy bear. But when he's out there competing, he puts the weight of the world on his shoulders because he's the guy who is getting all that money and it's a lot of pressure.

If his teammates aren't helping him out, Lester gets pissed. I told Jon he needed to communicate positivity and lift up his teammates. I've seen guys who are always negative, and it's hard to play with them.

A great teammate also shares what he's learned. It's a way of teaching the next generation of players. And I think that's such an important thing for the veterans. I mean, it's so much easier to do that as a veteran player who has a deeper perspective on things. I remember Rizzo was complaining about his swing earlier in the 2016 season and I was like, "Hey, try batting a buck-eighty for a year." I was being funny, but Anthony has always been open to my sharing the challenges of my long career, which I do only to help him keep his "challenges" in perspective.

Direct and early communication is a sign of great leadership. An example was when we traded for closer Aroldis Chapman in late July 2016. Before the Cubs acquired Chapman from the Yankees, President Theo Epstein talked to the veteran guys on our team and asked if we thought Chapman might negatively change the chemistry of the clubhouse. Chapman had been suspended by Major League Baseball for thirty games in the spring for violating MLB's domestic violence policy. There's no exact formula for team chemistry and human beings are complicated. There is no player who is a great teammate all the time, nor one who is always bad. It's not that simple. We're all combinations of good qualities and bad qualities and moods and our past history. As I showed, we can change and do better. Though none of the veterans on our team really knew Chapman, we all felt comfortable saying our locker room was so strong we knew he could meld with us. More than that, we appreciated Theo being direct and communicating with us what the team was planning to do. He is a model of great leadership.

Like Theo, what we really wanted was to add as much talent as we could with guys who care about their teammates, who are invested first and foremost in the outcome of the group, who are willing to control their own personal interests, and who give a shit. If you fill your roster with enough of those types of guys, you're probably going to have something good going on.

Problem Solving

Great teammates look for solutions without complaining. For me, it was about game calling behind the plate, trying to get the best situation for my pitcher. But everybody should be trying to help the group solve the big problem, which is, how we're going to win today. How are we going to beat our opponent? How are we going to put ourselves in the best situation to succeed as a group? Good teammates aren't focused just on their hits and plays, but on how what they do helps the collective. They can help their teammates succeed. They focus on helping other people solve the problem—no matter how big or how small.

Sacrifice

No task is beneath you. Sacrifice is for the betterment of the group. I might have been a veteran player on the roster, but if a teammate ripped his batting gloves and everyone on the bench was busy, I probably had the most time of anyone to help out. Even if that guy probably would have never said, "Hey, Rossy, go get me a pair of batting gloves," I didn't mind because whatever needed to be done, I did it.

Speaking of sacrifice, I always worked on my bunting. I was not a superstar, so I always worked on bunting because it's a skill that helps win games. It isn't glamorous and not everyone liked to bunt. I am sure we all have moments in a season or in a job that we are asked to do tasks that we might not be 100 percent committed to or feel that is maybe beneath us. But you have to step up and do them to help your team or your business be successful. That's life . . . as a teammate!

Doing a task without complaining is the best approach. It is not always easy and I'll admit I can complain with the best of them, but it is necessary to put the group in front of your own personal needs or wants to succeed.

Dealing with Change

When your goal is to win a championship in a highly competitive field, there are going to be bumps and challenges along the road. I think the guys who are able to adjust and keep their focus on moving forward no matter what the circumstances are the ones who will deal with change the best. And change is one constant in baseball. The game is built around managers making adjustments, often in the moment, to create advantage.

Joe Maddon said it best: "Trust the process because the process is fearless." There are going to be a lot of things that are out of your control but if you keep working at getting better to be the best version of you, the rest is just wasted emotion.

If I got sent down to the minors, I couldn't just feel sorry for myself. Nobody feels sorry for you in baseball. The game goes on whether you are part of the team or not. You have to deal with change and disappointment.

Great teammates can find that balance to continue to push forward and find a way to communicate through problems and changes. When a problem arises in life, make adjustments, find a positive in it, and make it the best day you can.

Engagement

In Boston, Dustin Pedroia was a huge influence in my life in terms of how he conducted himself. His intensity and focus. Every at-bat was important to Dustin. If he struck out in a 15–1 game in a situation where he thought he should have gotten a hit to help the team, he was pissed. (By the way, that's a true story . . . and we were winning!)

In Atlanta, Bobby Cox was as engaged as any leader I've seen. I sat next to Bobby and his coaching staff on the bench and listened to a lot of their conversations. I always seemed to find myself next to the managers. I always wanted to hear what they talked about during games.

Bobby was always thinking steps ahead of everyone else. Atlanta pitching coach Roger McDowell used to sit next to me and he'd ask, "What would you throw right here?" So I had to be locked in on every pitch. If I wasn't engaged in the game, I couldn't go pitch to pitch with him.

As a teammate, you have to stay invested in and engaged with the guys who are out there playing because that's the only way you are going to lift them up. Too many guys check out when they are not playing. I think that is totally wrong. I think the best teammates are the ones in the dugout watching the game from the bench and seeing exactly what is going on. If I criticized a teammate, they knew it wasn't out of the blue, because I was always watching. I had earned their trust because they knew I was watching and engaged in every game.

Being Positive

Bobby Cox was the master. Those years in Atlanta under Bobby as my manager really made me a lot better because I watched how he watched the field . . . and he watched everything that happened on the field. Say if the outfielder made a great catch for the first out, but then we gave up five runs in the inning. With most people, that great catch might be forgotten because everyone was down as they came off the field because we allowed a five-spot. But in situations like that, Bobby would walk down the dugout and pat that guy on the butt and say, "Nice catch." Bobby always focused on the positive aspect, even in a negative moment.

Accountability

Players—people, too—often want to make excuses when things go wrong. Not a great teammate. The truth is that none of us is perfect, and the best response when a mistake is made is to own it, to be accountable. Some people equate calling yourself out with being vulnerable. That may be true. I promise you that the minute you show vulnerability, I think that allows you to build trust. I feel like, Okay, now we are all on the same level. I made mistakes. I made a lot of them—and I still make them. I also try to hold myself accountable for them.

The reason that is so important is that you can't hold others accountable—which your teammates need from you—until you show the ability to hold yourself to a high standard.

I think players put so much pressure on themselves. After games, we had to answer to the media and talk about how and why something happened in the game, be it positive or negative. And there were times when players made excuses. But if I made a mistake and I owned it, what else was there to talk about?

As a player, if you make excuses or try to blame somebody else, all of a sudden it becomes a five-day story in the media. Being accountable nips that story right in the bud. I tried to diffuse situations. For instance, in Game One of the World Series, I don't think I called a very good game. Jon Lester didn't throw badly, but I just didn't set him up for as much success as he possibly could have had, in my opinion. And that's what I said following the game. There weren't many follow-up questions!

Being Social

Teammates have to get to know each other. As a player, I just can't know you in one aspect of your life. That was one of the things we did so well with the Cubs. I remember everyone got together in St. Louis after a game during my first year in Chicago. Players had a FIFA Xbox tournament going on. Heck, I don't even know how to turn on an Xbox. But it was great camaraderie building because everyone hung out and talked about things. You saw how players interacted with each other. Some guys were locked in on the Xbox, some guys shot the bull, some guys were on social media. But everyone was together and guys talked about different things and interacted. We had so many good personalities in the room, like Dexter Fowler and Anthony Rizzo, even young guys liken Addison Russell. Our good social time helped make the communication so much better and easy throughout the year.

Toughness

You just can't be the nice guy and pat everyone on the back. One of the coolest things I ever heard was from Dave Roberts when I was with the Dodgers and we were teammates. Somebody was giving him a hard time and he looked the guy right in the eye and said, "Don't mistake kindness for weakness." I have used it a lot because my being the nice guy and supporting guy doesn't mean you can take advantage of me or beat me down. We had a pitcher who threw some ice across the locker room and hit me in the head several times. He was just messing around but one time he hit me after a game in Arizona and I walked over to him and told him if he did it again, we were going to go at it. It was his last warning. He saw the seriousness in my face and we never had a problem again.

Trust

As players, you have to have each other's backs. Once when I was with Cincinnati, we were playing the Atlanta Braves, and Braves catcher Brian McCann—I didn't know Brian at the time—said something to one of our hitters, Jerry Hairston, when he tried to bunt in a game we were getting no-hit. I jumped off the bench and started yelling at Brian. I had no idea what they were talking about, but I stood up for my teammate.

I am going to be the first guy to say something; that's just the way I am. The Braves probably thought it was cheesy to try to bunt in that situation and, if I was on the Braves team, I might have thought the same. But I wasn't on their team. I was on my team. So right or wrong, I had to have Jerry's back. There are certain guys and teams in the league that want to police everything, and I think that's wrong. You play your game and we will play ours. Don't tell us how to play. We have to have each other's backs and teammates have to be able to trust each other. In the heat of the battle, I stuck up for my teammates.

Heck, my first year with the Cubs in 2015, I was ejected when I wasn't even in the game. We were playing the Reds and Dexter Fowler was at-bat. He checked his swing, but Paul Schrieber, the umpire, called it a strike. All I said to Schrieber was to get help on the call—to consult the ump working the line. Well, Paul walked to our bench and told Joe Maddon that he'd better "shut him up"—and he pointed at me.

Whoa! I said, "Listen, nobody is going to tell me to shut up, I am a grown-ass man." I lost it and said a few choice words before Paul ejected me. Was it worth it? Absolutely. Dexter thanked me later. He knew I had his back. When your teammates know that you have their back, they will trust you, and they will follow you.

Fun

A great teammate is someone whom others appreciate and want to be around. They have a good time. I always tried to have a good time when I played baseball, but I always wondered: What did people like about me? I never thought I was cool, but I made sure I had a good time on the field. That must have been it.

I always made fun of myself, too. That's my personality. Like with the "Grandpa Rossy" nickname. When it first came up, I willingly put on a "Grandpa Rossy" uniform and walked around with a walker and a cane. It was fun. It was easy for me to make fun of myself because I couldn't relate to what it's like to be a superstar.

One of my favorite quotes, from John Wooden, the late basketball coach for the University of California, Los Angeles, is "Be more concerned with your character than your reputation, because your character is what you really are, while your reputation is merely what others think you are." I have that quote framed at my house. At the end of the day, you know your strengths and weaknesses.

If I was the old guy, Grandpa Rossy, I was fine with that. It was fun. And it gave us something to laugh about as a team.

If someone wants to become a great teammate, however, they have to go back to the big lesson we scribbled on the whiteboard in the Braves' training room years ago: "Be Honest With Yourself." If someone goes through this list and isn't honest with himself, it would be tough for him to become the best teammate out there. It is important to know what you need to work on and you can only do that if you're honest with yourself.

CHAPTER 17

WRIGLEY

6 A.M.

W hen we landed in O'Hare and the flight taxied to a hangar, the city of Chicago was ready to welcome the World Series champion Cubs home!

Around two hundred airport employees cheered, clapped, and gave us a standing ovation as we deplaned and climbed aboard the buses that would drive us the fourteen miles to Wrigley Field. And as we got ready to exit the airport, Chicago Fire Department trucks saluted us with sprays of water from their hoses that cascaded over the buses. It was so cool. The buses headed down the Kennedy Expressway and people in their vehicles waved and honked their horns. The magic number to the World Series title was finally zero. It seemed so surreal. We understood how much this victory meant to Cubs fans. The excitement had seemed to build and build over the course of the season, and we were so happy for them.

Many fans who watched Game Seven from the bars and restaurants in Wrigleyville, near the field, had never gone home and so lined the streets as we arrived before sunrise. The stadium marquee at Wrigley Field was lit up with the words WORLD SERIES CHAMPI-ONS. Anthony Rizzo lifted the Commissioner's Trophy above his head when he got off the bus.

By the time we retrieved our luggage and found the Uber driver, all Hyla and I wanted to do was sleep. But not before we smiled over a funny ending to such a wonderful journey.

The Ross family piled into an Uber that actually was reserved for Theo Epstein. Then we took off.

Sorry, Theo.

. . . .

DAVID'S iPHONE JOURNAL
10/3/16

"Don't be sad that it's over, smile because it happened." —Vin Scully

. . . .

The party that was 108 years in the making lived up to its billing.

Chicago officials estimated about five million people—nearly twice the city's population, to make it the seventh-largest gathering in human history, according to media reports—attended the World Series celebration that featured a six-mile parade and rally from Wrigley Field to Grant Park on Friday, November 4, 2016, two days after we won Game Seven.

Friday was a scheduled day off for Chicago Public Schools, so the crowd seemed to be dominated by families and kids as we traveled the parade route on double-decker buses. Illinois governor Bruce Rauner declared "Word Champion Chicago Cubs Day" statewide. The Chicago River was dyed Cubs blue.

It was a beautiful, 60-degree sunny morning and it couldn't have been any better—even if I sliced the top of my nose on a wire that held a partition between us and the fans as we boarded the buses at Wrigley Field. I wasn't the only player wounded. John Lackey was cut across the neck and Travis Wood and Jon Lester were nicked atop their heads. While my flesh wound may have been the worst out of the bunch, I wasn't going to let a bloody cut ruin my day.

When we arrived at Hutchinson Field in Grant Park for the rally, Wayne Messmer, the longtime public address announcer for the Cubs sang the national anthem. Pat Hughes, the play-by-play voice of the Cubs Radio Network, introduced the brass—Cubs chairman Tom Ricketts and presidents Crane Kenney and Theo Epstein—as everyone gathered on the stage. After they all said a few words, including manager Joe Maddon, players had their turns.

I was fine emotionally until Rizzo started to talk about me. "He taught me how to become a real winner," Anthony said to the crowd as he got choked up. "He is like a brother to me. He has taught me a lot in life, on the field and off, how to be a better person. I am forever grateful for him. He's going out a champion forever. The last game he played in, he's a world champion."

I was next to speak, and I had all these things I planned to say about each one of my teammates. It was going to be quick, just something about each guy and how they made me better. I couldn't get any of it out because Rizz started tearing up and I choked up. I wanted to mention my wife and my kids, my mom and dad, and thank the boys for the trophy. Instead, basically all I had in me was, "I love these guys and I am out."

I was overcome by a wave of emotion. That's one of my problems. When I am passionate about something, I get emotional.
(Thanks, Mom!) It's hard for me to get my feelings across in words
because I tend to choke up. I really wanted each of the guys to
understand what they meant to me. In my mind, they don't get it.
They had no idea how they affected me—and how incredibly grateful I was that they treated me the way they did.

I was the backup catcher and the whole journey still blows my
mind. I get carried off the field after Game Seven? I mean, really? I
was the lowest-paid veteran on the roster, I played once a week, and
they treated me like an MVP. Everyone said it was because I meant
so much to them. But I was just being me. That made me wonder
exactly who they were talking about. I am a guy who has flaws, but
I always worked to be honest with myself. We all have flaws. I don't
know what I am but I do know it was so cool when all those things
happened to a guy like me.

Even though I was often described by the Chicago media as
a "personal catcher" to Jon Lester, it really never bothered me.
Reporters always asked me why I worked so well together with
Jon, and that was something I never had an answer for. I felt like I
worked well with every pitcher I caught once I was given the opportunity to learn his strengths and weaknesses. You do that when
you catch them regularly. But I wasn't a good enough hitter or a
good enough player to play every day to have that opportunity with
every pitcher on a staff. I felt like the manager decided, "Okay, you
are really good at this and you give us a good chance to win when
you're paired with this guy." That was the goal: to win every game
when I was behind the plate.

Theo Epstein has often said that when he was a staff member
with the San Diego Padres in the mid-1990s he learned a lesson on

the importance of being honest, from former player Craig Shipley. Shipley said, "Theo, don't you get it? Every single player in every clubhouse in the big leagues has either been lied to by management or expects to be." It shocked Theo and he never forgot it as he started to gain more responsibility in the game.

He believed that if an organization could create a culture where players knew they were being told the truth, it would be a big competitive advantage and would help nurture great relationships and a great environment where players could relax and be confident and be themselves around management. Put building trust and acting with integrity on the same level as winning. If you can find that equilibrium and that environment, really good things follow.

When Theo moved to the Red Sox in 2002, he incorporated that mindset and blueprint. Then, six years later, as I was packing my bags after that short 2008 stint in Boston, Theo used the lesson he had learned from Craig Shipley to change my career. He spoke honestly with me about what he had heard about my departure from Cincinnati. That level of candor, which he promised to bring to any team he led, changed my career and was part of what brought us back together in Chicago.

The rest is history!

◇

The November weekend after Game Seven was a blur. Following the parade and rally on Friday, Anthony Rizzo, Dexter Fowler, and I joined actor Bill Murray, a die-hard Cubs fan, on *Saturday Night Live* in New York City. It all was in good fun, but I am not sure people (including my family!) were prepared to see me as a male stripper, which was the skit they handed us. And I didn't want to embarrass my daughter with my dance moves. Rizz, Dexter, and I strip-teased for a grandmother, who, in the skit, had possibly died due to a heart attack. Naturally, we were dressed in Cubs-themed stripper attire.

"Don't worry, Grandma, Grandpa Rossy is here to take care of you," was my infamous line before I climbed on the back of the chair for our "triple-header," as Rizz told the audience. Near the end of the show we, along with Murray, crashed *SNL*'s "Weekend Update" disguised as winners of the mock news show's *The Voice*-type contest. We sang a rendition of the Cubs' unofficial anthem, "Go Cubs, Go." It was fun but kind of a blur.

From there we flew back to Chicago, where I joined Jason Heyward, Kyle Schwarber, and Mike Montgomery at the Chicago Blackhawks' hockey game at the United Center Sunday night. At intermission, I played "Shoot the Puck" but missed on all three of my attempts. On Monday I flew to Los Angeles and appeared on *The Ellen DeGeneres Show* with Kris Bryant. I was presented with a Grandpa Rossy walker, which I needed when I caught the red-eye back to Chicago because we had to pack and be out of our apartment by midweek.

It was time to get home to Tallahassee.

Hyla and I had a plan for when I retired. Or so we thought. Everything that had happened over the course of the 2016 season, culminating in the World Series victory, had turned our lives upside down. Everything happened so quickly we barely had time to wrap our heads and hands around all that was coming at us.

Hyla felt like we crossed the finish line, as we had planned—that was our goal for so many years—but I know it suddenly felt like Hyla crossed it alone. She looked around and I was gone, back on an airplane and traveling the country. We actually sat down and revamped our future plans a bit, mainly because all these good things had happened to us. I could have never envisioned it. My itinerary, for instance, in the first three months following our Series title included an event at a Dick's Sporting Goods store in Chicago where I signed 1,256 autographs; I partnered with Duracell to deliver batteries to Toys for Tots Chicago for Christmas; my son, Cole, and I participated in a father-son competition ("Big Star, Little Star") that was taped in Los Angeles and will be televised by the USA Network; Public Label Brands Inc. featured me on a limited edition collector's box for a cereal called "Grandpa Rossy" Crunch; I was the keynote speaker at the University of St. Francis's annual fund-raiser in Joliet, Illinois, and my Florida High basketball coach, Al Blizzard, attended as a guest of the university. My 2017 calendar may feature more road dates than a baseball season!

Children, of course, have a way to put everything in perspective.

In late November 2016, I headed to Maclay School and picked up Cole and Landri. On the way home, Landri, who is in the fourth grade, innocently asked from the backseat, "Dad, now that you don't have a job anymore, do you think you could coach PE at Maclay?"

That's the line everyone fears, right? "Dad, now that you don't have a job anymore." I smiled inside and probably even laughed.

David Ross, PE coach.

I told Landri she probably didn't want me around her school every day.

EPILOGUE

From backup catcher to A-list celebrity? It still cracks me up. But within sixty days of that last game in my career, Ryan, my agent, informed me that I had crossed some strange threshold and my story had put me in the "A-list" category. Me? Not possible!

There was a time when I wondered what I'd do after I retired as a player in the major leagues. But, of course, the 2016 season with the Chicago Cubs changed my life beyond belief. I have to give the credit to my teammates, the Cubs organization, and Cubs fans everywhere. Where does a role player get this much attention? How do I go from the baseball dugout to *Dancing with the Stars*? It's a script that would have been tossed out for being just too unrealistic.

My success—and the reason I could even write a book like this—came because others invested in me. Guys like Brian McCann and Dave Roberts; college coaches Hal Baird and Andy Lopez; general managers Kevin Towers and Wayne Krivsky; all the managers and players, all the people beyond even the ones I've mentioned in this book. Each of them has affected my life in positive ways they don't even know. They changed me as a person and what I believe in, what I value as important, what winning is, and what being a good person is. Everything that we've talked about in this book is because the people I've met have changed my mindset and made me better. I feel like I've stolen a piece from thousands of folks and made it my own. I owned my behavior and, at the end of my career, I've gotten all this love. That's crazy. But I also feel there's so much more to go and so much more growth in who I will become. I'm closing a chapter in my life, but I am not closing the book.

I want to be a great husband and a great dad, so how do I do that? What does that look like? I want to be excited about my kids' events and still show them that Dad works hard. This is what Dad believes in. This is the example that Dad is going to set. And these are the qualities that Dad expects out of me. I want to see that play out, whatever else happens in my life.

For my entire life I have enjoyed being out of my comfort zone. I want to continually test myself. That's how you learn, right? On January 13, 2017, the Cubs named me as a special assistant to baseball operations. I joked I was the organization's newest intern. Honestly, as I write this in February 2017, I still don't even know what I'm going to be doing exactly. I expect it to be a learning process and the Cubs offered me the opportunity to grow in my baseball knowledge and try to learn different aspects of what goes on in the organization. I will have my fingers in a number of different elements, from scouting to working within the front office. I was also hired by ESPN as an MLB analyst. The network announced I would provide analysis on *SportsCenter*, in the studio, and even join some game broadcasts. I worked with ESPN as an analyst during the postseason in 2014 and 2015 and really enjoyed it.

Working for the Cubs and for ESPN were easy decisions. Agreeing to join the twenty-fourth season of *Dancing with the Stars* on ABC took some thought. Initially I wasn't really keen on the idea, but the more I thought about it, the more I figured, Why not? If stepping outside my comfort zone was a theme, why not dance outside it? I was told by the show's producers that I was the first professional baseball player ever to compete, but more important, they convinced me it would be fun. They said my personality was perfect for the show because I don't take myself seriously, and the show, despite the competition, doesn't take itself too seriously.

I knew that former professional football player and Hall of Famer Emmitt Smith was winner of season three with Cheryl Burke, and it changed his life forever. Hall of Fame receiver Jerry Rice finished second on season two and the experience introduced him to people all over the country and the world who never realized he played professional football. I mean, this is a guy who's widely considered to be the greatest wide receiver in NFL history. And here I am, a backup catcher! Who would believe it? I told ABC yes, and I started Pilates classes to help with my flexibility and posture, just in case! I didn't have any expectations for myself, but I was looking forward to the experience.

I look back on my baseball career and I still pinch myself. Players like me might get lost in the shuffle because the game has changed and analytics are so important. Character matters, too, not just numbers. Cubs president Theo Epstein said his appreciation has grown for how much the human element matters and how much winning-focused players can impact the rest of the team and create something that's maybe immeasurable but also valuable.

For the same reason that a pitcher's velocity might be overvalued—he throws hard but his fastball doesn't have any movement and he's hit all over the park—maybe to some degree a player's track record is incorrectly taken into consideration. It's hard to incorporate as a core element of your team-building philosophy, but it's incredibly important. There are a lot of talented teams year after year that don't win because they might have too many selfish players and don't have the players who are conscious of building the right environment. I would never go as far as to say it's more important than talent. Obviously, you need the talent to begin with, but talent alone isn't enough.

That's what we accomplished as World Series champions in 2016 with the Chicago Cubs and in 2013 with the Boston Red Sox. I am so thankful I was able to play fifteen years in the major leagues. I evolved as a player, as a teammate, and as a man.

But I am no different than anyone else.

I just always thought of myself as a regular guy who had a pretty cool job.

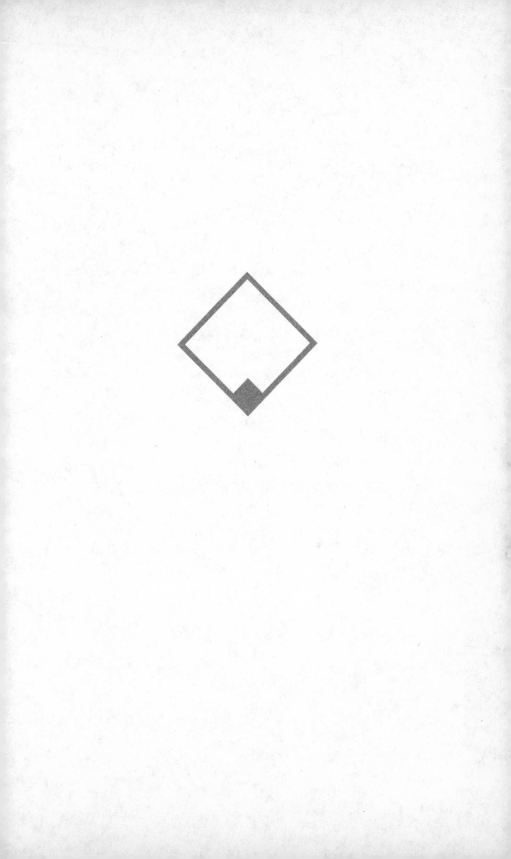

ACKNOWLEDGMENTS

A book like this would not have been possible without . . . an incredible team! Like my career, this book doesn't happen without the energy, hard work, dedication, assistance, and support of a host of others.

I have to start with my rock: My wife, Hyla, has been supportive at every step and worked so hard on pulling together photos for the book. My kids, Landri, Cole, and Harper, were willing to give up some "daddy time" so I could give this project the attention it deserved.

I also want to thank my parents, Jackie and David, and many teammates and coaches for their support and sharing their stories and memories—and for not humiliating me in the process! Ian Kleinert, the agent for this book, was absolutely fantastic and worked with my longtime friend and baseball agent, Ryan Gleichowski, to find the best publisher for this work. I was initially reluctant about writing a book and Ian helped me understand the process. The

writing team of Don Yaeger and Jim Henry were so well prepared—
and I should have expected nothing less from Jim, who has been
a family friend for years. Because we were working on such tight
deadlines, Don and Jim engaged a wonderful line editor, Jeremy
Elliott, who spent hours poring over every word. And thanks to Bill
Swales Jr. for all the amazing research he did to keep this project in
perspective.

Paul Whitlatch, our incredible editor at Hachette Books, saw
this project as bigger than even I did, right from the beginning.

We also found several resources to be especially helpful in
reconstructing certain scenes and checking numbers. The good
folks at Baseball-Reference.com run a top-notch site that not only
posts player stats, but also has features like an online video on how
to read a play-by-play. It is an awesome resource for any baseball
fan or sportswriter.

The print, online, and broadcast media in Chicago and nation-
ally provided comprehensive coverage of our 2016 season, and there
were so many outlets that provided some great articles and analysis
that were very helpful in pulling this project together. That lengthy
list of writers includes Carrie Muskat and Jon Heyman at MLB.
com, Tom Verducci at *Sports Illustrated,* Buster Olney, Peter Gam-
mons, Tim Kurkjian at ESPN, Bob Nightengale at *USA Today,* Ken
Rosenthal at Fox Sports, Paul Sullivan and Tim Bannon at the *Chicago Tribune,* and Chris De Luca at the *Chicago Sun-Times,* among
many others.